The Most Terrible Pogrom in History

Daniel Farcas

Published by Daniel Farcas, 2023.

THE MOST TERRIBLE POGROM IN HISTORY

First edition. December 5, 2023.

Copyright © 2023 Daniel Farcas.

ISBN: 979-8223845737

Written by Daniel Farcas.

Dedication

It is impossible to name them all, but symbolically I want to highlight the leaders of the Jewish Community of Chile, in representation of all those who work on this difficult task. These include its former president, Gabriel Zaliasnik, and its current board headed by Ariela Agosin accompanied by Gabriel Silber, Daphne Englander, and Grace Agosin.

I also want to acknowledge the individuals and organizations around the world who work successfully to combat anti-Semitism, such as Angel Mas and the incredible work of Acom in Spain, the important broadcast of radio Sefarad, the persistence of Miguel Steuerman on Radio Jai, and the notable effort of Aurora with the leadership of Federico.

The community of Chileans in Israel also does extraordinary work led by Gabriel with the support of Hernan Lopez and Sivan Giborn. In Israel, the perseverance in the permanent quality work of Ron Brummer, the effort and effectiveness of many academic academics represented in Doctor Michael Ehrlich, and the support that Bar Ilan University has given me is commendable.

I would like to express my gratitude to Rony Kaplan and Gabriel Chocron for helping those who visit Israel understand and learn more about the Middle East. I also want to thank Revitale Einstein and Natalia Sidon. It is impossible to name them all, but symbolically I want to highlight the leaders of the Jewish Community of Chile, in representation of all those who work on this difficult task. These include its former president, Gabriel Zaliasnik, and its current board headed by Ariela Agosin accompanied by Gabriel Silber, Daphne Englander, and Grace Agosin.

I also want to acknowledge the individuals and organizations around the world who work successfully to combat anti-Semitism, such as Angel Mas and the incredible work of Acom in Spain, the important broadcast of radio Sefarad, the persistence of Miguel Steuerman on Radio Jai, and the notable effort of Aurora with the leadership of Federico

The community of Chileans in Israel also does extraordinary work led by Gabriel with the support of Hernan Lopez and Sivan Giborn. In Israel, the perseverance in the permanent quality work of Ron Brummer, the effort and effectiveness of many academic academics represented in Doctor Michael Ehrlich, and the support that Bar Ilan University has given me is commendable.

I would like to express my gratitude to Rony Kaplan and Gabriel Chocron for helping those who visit Israel understand and learn more about the Middle East. I also want to thank Revitale Einstein, Natalia Sidon, and Ella Mirzaib from the Abdorcion Ministry for their trust and permanent encouragement.

I am grateful for the Israeli parliamentarians who care about the diaspora, such as Shareen Eskel, and for the hundreds of parliamentarians around the world who choose to defend the just cause of the only democracy in the Middle East. In particular, I want to acknowledge those who belong to the progressive sector, who are often misrepresented by those with an anti-Israeli agenda. This includes my great friend Mr. Jaime Quintana and the former president of the Chamber of Deputies of Chile, Marco Nuñez.

I cannot fail to mention two exceptional communicators, Luciano Mondino and Pilar Rahola. The list is endless, and I hope it continues to lengthen. the Absorcion ministry for their trust and permanent encouragement. We have been living for more than two years in the fantastic city of Netanya, and the major is doing great and is absolutely committed to facing the huge challenge of Middle-Eastern misinformation. Thank you Míriam Feiberg

I am grateful for the Israeli

I cannot fail to mention two exceptional communicators, Luciano Mondino and Pilar Rahola. The list is endless, and I hope it continues to lengthen.

And the last ones are the most important, my great family. My father Alberto and my mother Clara, my brothers David, Alan and Claudia, my wife Pamela and all the greatnew generation that will be even beter

Thanks to all of you!

ByAngel Mas[1]
President of Action and Communication in the Middle East (ACOM).

On October 7, 2023, the most inhumane massacre imaginable that left 1,400 dead, 4,000 injured and 240 kidnapped reminded us in the most cruel way of some truths that, in the false security of our prosperity, in the heat of an apparent and civilized coexistence, We had not wanted to confront for decades:

That the true face of our enemies is brutal, insatiable, genocidal. What is evil in its purest form and, therefore, only its total, devastating and incontestable defeat can be acceptable.

We woke up to our own vulnerability, to the fragility of the safe home we thought we had in Israel, especially in the face of a savage enemy that has no limits. And to defend it, we will not only be able to depend on technology. Human sacrifices will be necessary.

We discover the dream of our own prosperity. It is why we had convinced ourselves of the serious problems that our society had. All of them today seem as distant as they are frivolous and banal. Our bitter arguments have proven completely irrelevant when reality has hit us.

We also had to accept, not only that the two-state solution will never be, since a large part of the Palestinians do not want their state, but to end ours, that a very important segment of the Palestinian population probably unrecoverable for any coexistence, their brutality has no solution.

They helped us remember that the Muslim world has a sick, compulsive, irrational and truly violent hatred against us. The dehumanization of the Jew has triumphed in their culture. There is no empathy, whatever happens to us. We are guilty, whatever we do.

One of the most painful observations was the amount of hatred projected against the Jews by all those who have made their anti-Semitism a fashion. Acquired, intellectualized, supervened. Which is born from fictitious grievances of a story as prevalent as it is fallacious. And that infects a very important part of the population, our neighbors, who are tremendously dedicated to spreading this violent hatred.

We know that anti-Semitism / anti-Zionism in Western countries is the most visible symptom of a serious problem of disaffection of a part of their citizens with their own democracies, with the values of freedom and guarantees, hatred of their own well-being. And projecting all this against the Jewish State and against the Jews has mutated into a contagious and socially acceptable fashion.

In case there were any doubts, we note that international institutions such as the United Nations cannot be counted on at all, that the double standards against Israel and the cynicism of a large part of the international community are irrecoverable, and that the rest of the accidental countries will offer their formal sympathy and solidarity while they continue to finance the criminals who beheaded children, raped women, burned families, tortured children in front of their parents, murdered parents in front of their children and kidnapped 240 people, some of them babies.

We have harshly remembered, in short, that we cannot lose any war, because it would be the last. That we only have to count on ourselves to defend ourselves. And listen very little to the complaints of those who do not seem to tolerate the fact that Jews do not allow themselves to be slaughtered for free. That appeasement and containment were a mistake. That our enemies only seek our total destruction and are deeply committed to achieving that goal. And that is why our only option is a decisive victory that destroys them, at least for a generation.

---

1.   https://elmed.io/author/angel-mas/

Thanks and aknoledge

Writing this book was a tough experience, especially as it coincided with the Simchat Torah war, which originated from the abhorrent and monstrous acts carried out by the Hamas-ISIS terrorist group. I am immensely grateful to the following individuals and organizations who have played a crucial role in the creation of this book:

Firstly, I would like to express my deep appreciation to Bar Ilan University, particularly Professor Michael Ehrlich, for their support and guidance. Additionally, I am grateful to the Jewish Agency, especially Revitale Einstein and Natalia Sidon, for their contributions. The directors of the Jewish Community of Chile, Ariela Agosin, Daphne Englander, Gabriel Silber, and Grace Agosin, have also been instrumental in this endeavor.

I would like to extend my heartfelt thanks to the board of directors of the Community of Chileans in Israel, namely Gabriel Colodro, Hernan López, Daniel Weinstein, and especially Sivan Gobrin, for their invaluable support.

A special mention goes to my wife, Pamela Werbin, whose help and unwavering support have been indispensable throughout this process. I must also acknowledge Denisse Mahias, for her assistance in editing the book, as well as Dariela Farcas, the creator of the cover design. Furthermore, I am grateful to my mother, Clara Guendelman, for her translation assistance.

I would also like to emphasize my family's commitment to Israel. My parents, Alberto and Clara, and my siblings, David, Alan, and Claudia, have consistently set an example of dedication and unwavering efforts in support of Israel. I am confident that the next generation will continue this legacy and make an even greater impact.

Moreover, I want to express my gratitude to individuals like Ron Brumner, who spearheads the fight against new antisemitism and the BDS movement. Miriam Feiberg, the mayor of Netanya, has been a significant advocate for a better Jewish state.

In the academic sphere, Lesley Kleef's outstanding work at Leeds University, particularly her leading role in combating antisemitism, deserves special mention.

In the field of communications, I deeply appreciate leaders like Miguel Steuerman in Argentinean radio Jai and Federico Treguer in Mexico, who leads the newspaper Aurora, for their efforts in explaining Israel's position.

Lastly, I want to acknowledge individuals who are not of Jewish descent but are working diligently in an increasingly antisemitic environment in Spain. Thank you to Pilar Rahola and Luciano Mondino for teaching us a valuable lesson in unwavering commitment.

I extend my sincere thanks once again to all those mentioned and anyone else who has contributed to this book.

Chapter 1: Anti-Semitism in history: the terrible and painful past of the Jewish people

Anti-Semitism has been a sad reality, which has marked an important part of the history of the Jewish people.

Analyzing and understanding the roots, manifestations and consequences of this form of discrimination, as well as highlighting the importance of eradicating it in today's society, is a moral imperative.

Anti-Semitism has its roots in antiquity, reaching its peak during the Middle Ages and World War II. During the Middle Ages, Jews were subject to persecution and expulsions in Europe, being accused of being responsible for the death of Jesus and of conspiring against Christians. These unfounded accusations led to the creation of Jewish ghettos and the enactment of discriminatory laws.

A long and terrible experience was the constant persecutions and expulsions. The darkest points in the history of anti-Semitism are found in the Inquisition and in the last century, in the Holocaust, in which six million Jews were murdered by the Nazi regime. This genocide left an indelible mark on the history and collective memory of the Jewish people. The Holocaust is irrefutable proof of the cruelty and hatred that can arise when anti-Semitism is allowed to take root in a society.

Anti-Semitism has not only manifested itself in acts of physical violence, but also in social, economic and political discrimination. Over the centuries, Jews have been excluded from certain jobs, denied access to education, and unfairly blamed for economic and political problems. These discriminatory attitudes have perpetuated negative stereotypes and generated a climate of hatred and distrust towards the Jewish people.

From ancient times to the Holocaust, Jews have been victims of discrimination, persecution and genocide.

The truth is that every crisis in the Middle East proves him right. According to Bernard Henry Levy, "Anti-Semitism is a poison that spreads through different contexts and justifications, but always has the same result: the demonization and persecution of Jews. To deny this is not only ignorant, but also dangerous. (72)

Richard L. Rubinstein argues that anti-Semitism is rooted in human history and has manifested itself in different ways over the centuries. Rubinstein argues that hostility toward Jews is based on a combination of religious, economic, and political factors, and has resurfaced in times of geopolitical upheaval, such as conflicts in the Middle East.

And by the way, it is worth remembering, a powerful voice in the fight against anti-Semitism. Elie Wiesel, Holocaust survivor and winner of the Nobel Peace Prize, dedicated his life to remembering and denouncing the horrors of the Jewish genocide, and warned about the importance of always being attentive to any manifestation of hatred and discrimination towards Jews.

Deborah Lipstadt correctly states, "Intolerance has always existed, but we have never legitimized it as much as we are doing today. Hate words and speech have real consequences, and anti-Semitism is no exception." (73)

Education and the promotion of tolerance are key tools to combat this form of discrimination. It is necessary to foster respect for all people, regardless of their religion or ethnicity, and promote equal rights and opportunities for all.

It is urgent to learn from the mistakes of the past and work together to build a future in which all people are treated with dignity and respect.

Chapter 2: Islam, different visions and interpretations

Islam and its Anti-Jewish Roots

Islam is a monotheistic religion that originated in the 7th century in the Arabian Peninsula. Throughout their history, there have been tensions and conflicts between Islam and Judaism.

Some argue that Islam has anti-Jewish roots, while others maintain that these tensions are the result of historical and political factors after its origins. In this essay, it will be argued that Islam has anti-Jewish roots based on historical and theological evidence.

The first argument that Islam has anti-Jewish roots is based on the treatment of Jews at the time of the Prophet Muhammad. Although Muhammad initially sought cooperation with the Jews, relations quickly deteriorated.

In the city of Medina, Muhammad expelled two Jewish tribes and executed members of a third tribe. These historical events demonstrate a hostile attitude towards the Jews on the part of the prophet of Islam.

Furthermore, the Quran, the holy book of Islam, contains passages that can be interpreted as anti-Jewish. For example, he mentions the Jews as "those who have incurred the wrath of Allah" and "those who have gone astray."

Another argument is based on history after the time of Muhammad. During the Middle Ages, Jews in Islamic territories were subjected to restrictions and discrimination. For example, they were forced to wear badges to identify them and were prohibited from holding certain public positions.

These negative references contribute to the perception that Islam has an unfavorable view towards Jews, but in reality it is against infidels, that is, those who do not profess the faith of Islam.

This "detail" that seems to be overlooked by Christians and non-believers and that should matter to the progressive world anyway, is ignored or frankly deliberately omitted.

A reminder to the leftist world, there is no room for any progressive option or any of its causes in the world of Islam.

The pro-Jewish Islamic interpretation: Ahmadiyya

Islam is a religion that has been subject to diverse interpretations throughout history. One of them is pro-Jewish, pro-Israeli, pro-peace with the whole world, so much so that currently Imam Marwan Guill is a member, together with Miguel Steuerman, director of Jai radio, of the Argentine Jewish Muslim Confraternity, which seeks promote peaceful coexistence between Muslims and Jews.

Ahmadiyya argues that Islam and Judaism share many similarities and common values. Both religions believe in a single God and the importance of social justice. Furthermore, the Quran recognizes the Jews as "People of the Book", which implies a recognition of their religious and cultural heritage. Mirza Masroor Ahmad (مرزا مسرور احمد; born September 15, 1950) is the current and fifth leader of the Ahmadiyya Muslim Community. His official title within the movement is Fifth Caliph of the Messiah (Arabic: خليفة المسيح الخامس, khalīfatul masīh al-khāmis).

Mizra Masroor Amhad advocates respect for all religions and also highlights the importance of the city of Jerusalem for both religions. Both Muslims and Jews consider Jerusalem to be a sacred place of great spiritual significance. He argues that it is essential to promote peaceful coexistence in this city and respect the rights of all the religious communities that inhabit it.

Chapter 3: The pogroms: The horror against the Jewish people

The pogroms have been one of the darkest and most tragic episodes in the history of the Jewish people. These acts of violence and persecution have left an indelible mark on the collective memory of this community. In this essay, I will argue that the pogroms were a manifestation of hatred and prejudice towards Jews, and that their study and understanding are essential to prevent their repetition in the future.

Pogroms, which took place primarily in Eastern Europe during the 19th and 20th centuries, were violent, organized attacks against Jewish communities. These acts of violence were perpetrated by groups of people who, motivated by hatred and intolerance, sought to harm and destroy Jews. They were characterized by looting, arson, rape and murder, leaving a trail of destruction and suffering in their wake.

The origin of the pogroms lies in the discrimination and anti-Semitism rooted in European society at the time. Jews were considered "the other", a threat to the identity and values of the majority community. This negative view was based on unfounded stereotypes and prejudices, which portrayed Jews as usurers, conspirators, and enemies of the Christian faith.

In addition to religious intolerance, pogroms were also motivated by economic and political factors. Jews, in many cases, were seen as competition in the commercial and financial sphere, which generated resentment and envy. Furthermore, in times of political or social crisis, Jews were used as scapegoats, blaming them for the problems and difficulties society faced.

The violence not only affected the direct victims, but also had a devastating impact on Jewish communities as a whole. These virulent acts generated fear and mistrust, forcing Jews to live in constant fear for their safety and well-being. Many Jews were forced to leave their homes and emigrate to other countries in search of safety and a better life.

It is essential to study and understand pogroms to prevent their repetition in the future. Through knowledge and empathy, we can eventually eradicate hate and ensure a future where attacks on Jews are just a sad memory of the past.

The pogroms against the Jews in Palestine before and after the creation of the State of Israel

We Jews have lived uninterruptedly in what is now Israel for more than 3,000 years, despite the massacres and expulsions, since Abraham left Ur to reach the land of Israel. From that moment on, Jews have always lived in the land of Israel, despite the countless conquests, expulsions, massacres, exiles and many other hardships suffered by the Jewish people in this land.

It is important to note that the name Palestine was given to Judea as a punishment to the Jews for the uprisings against the Roman Empire; that is how since the year 63 BCE to 313 CE, the Roman Empire rules the land that is today Israel and yesterday was Judea, changing the name of Judea to Palestine and prohibiting Jewish life in Jerusalem (70 CE). However, we Jews continue to always try to maintain our national identity in the rest of the country, despite the expulsion edicts and of course in exile. It is very important to understand that the Palestinian identity emerged long after the creation of the state of Israel and while much of the territories that the Palestinians claim today were dominated and administered by the Arab countries that border Israel, there was no attempt to create a Palestinian state, that is the truth. The Palestinian Liberation Terrorist Organization (PLO) itself was created in 1964.

In this sense, it is time to get serious and end the Western fantasy that Israel does have a partner for peace, because that is simply not true. Who will be that partner? That terrorist who calls his parents from a kibbutz in southern Israel and tells them exultantly that he is calling from the cell phone of one of the ten Jews he has just murdered with his bare hands. His voice of joy and excitement at the "achievement achieved", while encouraging him to kill more Jews. What peace can be made with the Palestinians who came in to rape, rob, murder, torture and generate the greatest possible pain? And this It is not only suitable for the Hamas terrorists, but particularly for those Palestinian families, some of whom had worked in the kibbutzim, and who went so far as to kidnap and murder their former employers. Is that a partner for peace?

What happened on Saturday, October 7, was a pogrom in which Hitler's followers proved to be good students of the Nazi teachers, and it is time for Europe in particular, and the Western world in general, to understand that what happened in southern Israel It could happen in each and every city in Europe and the Western world in general.

The reflection is first that this great and bloody pogrom has precedents and history, and is in fact anchored in the long sequence of persecutions and attacks by Arabs and Muslims against the Jews, both in the land of Israel and in the diaspora.

In these true nightmares of blood, terror, rape, torture, humiliation, looting and arson, thousands of Jews were brutally murdered. The sin of the victims was the same as today, the crime or serious offense: being Jewish.

Before the creation of the State of Israel, pogroms against Jews in Palestine were relatively frequent. During the British Mandate period, which spanned from 1920 to 1948, anti-Jewish riots intensified. A prominent example is the Hebron massacre in 1929, where an Arab mob attacked and murdered innocent Jews in the city of Hebron. This pogrom left 67 Jews dead and many others injured.

The creation of the State of Israel has marked a significant change in the protection and security of the Jewish community. Although conflicts between Arabs and Jews persist, pogroms had become less frequent and less serious, until October 7, 2023, when the worst nightmare of this type suddenly occurred in southern Israel, leaving behind 241 kidnapped and more than 1400 dead (as of the date this book is being written, and which I will describe in more detail later).

Between 1918 and 1928, led by the Mufti of Jerusalem, Haj Amin al Husseini, the fire of hatred of Jews was fueled, generating pogroms regularly in Sefad, Jerusalem and many cities, farms and kibbutzim.

After the creation of the State of Israel, Pogroms were replaced by terrorist actions such as blowing up buses, pizzerias or nightclubs. Hamas-Isis and Islamic Jihad openly support terrorism, with the Palestinian Authority being theoretically more ambivalent, but in practice it is known to endorse violence, paying financial rewards, such as lifelong pensions, to those who carry out terrorist acts against Jews.

These events have been instigated by Arab leaders and are based on the false belief that Jews were usurping their lands and threatening their cultural and religious identity. Furthermore, increasing Jewish immigration to Palestine, fueled by Zionism, generated tensions and resentments between the Arab and Jewish communities. However, there was never theft of land, in fact the "Keren Kayemet le Israel", a global institution that collects resources to raise the existence of the State of Israel, gathered them, just as it does today. The Jewish Fund purchased thousands of hectares, which were basically desert or swamps, and which were later converted into a garden.

Furthermore, the State of Israel has demonstrated its commitment to human rights and equality for all its citizens, regardless of religion or ethnicity. This has contributed to the creation of a more inclusive and tolerant society, where pogroms and violence against Jews are condemned and legally prosecuted.

The second reflection on this massacre is that although it is happening today with Israel, however, Europe, the United States, Latin America, Australia and many others have already suffered Islamic terrorism firsthand. What happened in Israel in October 2023 is one more warning for Western society, as we know it. By the way, there is no possibility that someone who does not want to see and listen can understand the depth of what happened and the implications of it for the development of life in the West.

Chapter 4: The tyrannical regime of Iran: support and financing of terrorism, murder of homosexuals, and oppression of women, starting with those who do not wear the hijab

The Iranian regime has come under fire for its support and financing of terrorism, as well as its systematic violation of human rights. In particular, the persecution and murder of people belonging to the LGBTQ+ community and the oppression of women who do not wear the hijab have been highlighted.

By analyzing and exposing the evidence that supports these accusations, the tyrannical nature of the Iranian regime is demonstrated.

Support and financing of terrorism

Iran has been repeatedly accused of supporting and financing terrorist groups around the world. Organizations such as Hezbollah in Lebanon and Hamas in Palestine have received financial and military support from the Iranian regime. These groups have carried out numerous terrorist attacks, causing the deaths of thousands of innocent people.

Iran trains the Hamas-Isis army. In addition to funding them, Iran provides Hamas with advanced weaponry, military training, cybersecurity, and expertise in manufacturing military equipment inside Gaza. Hamas now has a naval commando unit and a standing army of 40,000 men.

Since October 7, Iran has provided support to Hamas by using Hezbollah, another army under its control, to bomb Israel from Lebanon. With two borders to defend, Israel sees its resources limited and its population severely traumatized.

A prominent example of how the tyrannical Iranian regime operates are the terrorist attacks on the Israeli embassy (1992) and the Argentine Israelite Mutual Association (AMIA) in 1994, in which 85 people died and more than 300 were injured. Investigations point to the participation of Hezbollah, with the support of Iran, in the planning and execution of these attacks. These cases are just one of many examples that demonstrate Iran's role in financing and supporting international terrorism.

Homosexual murder

The LGBTQ+ community in Iran faces systematic and brutal persecution. Homosexuality is considered a crime and is punishable by the death penalty. LGBTQ+ people are arrested, tortured, and executed for their sexual orientation. These practices clearly violate fundamental human rights and demonstrate the intolerance and lack of respect for diversity in the Iranian regime.

The oppression of women who do not wear the hijab

The Iranian regime imposes strict regulations on women's clothing, requiring the mandatory wearing of the hijab. Those women who decide not to use it are subject to persecution, harassment and violence. The morality police, known as "Gasht-e Ershad", patrol the streets to ensure that women comply with Islamic dress standards imposed by the regime.

This imposition of the hijab violates women's fundamental right to freedom of expression and to decide about their own bodies. Furthermore, it reinforces gender inequality and perpetuates discrimination against women in Iranian society.

The international community needs to take action to condemn and pressure the Iranian regime to respect human rights and put an end to these violations. The fight against terrorism and the defense of human rights must be priorities on the global agenda, and the Iranian regime must be held accountable for its actions. The incredible hypocrisy of progressivism and the left in general, with an unusual double standard, runs and rushes to condemn Israel for actions that the Jewish State did not commit, such as the Gaza hospital that was proven to have been bombed by the Islamic

Jihad, but it maintains a stony silence in the face of the murder of homosexuals and the lack of women's rights in the Islamic republic of Iran.

Chapter 5: Hezbollah. The party of God, its idiosyncrasies and its global threat

The Shiite terrorist organization Hezbollah has unfortunately been a successful experiment that has managed to combine religious fanaticism, military discipline and political influence.

The Lebanese terrorist group is a fundamental actor in that country's politics and maintains a substantive influence in all spheres of power, which positions it as a key actor in the Middle East.

The emergence of Hezbollah has its roots in the religious and political movements of the late 1960s and early 1970s that united Lebanese Shiites before the Lebanese Civil War.

The group has been classified as terrorist by the US and is included on the European Union's list of terrorist organizations. Also in the Organization of American States (OAS) and many other countries.

The Telemundo network states that "the United States accuses him of being responsible for the attack on the American Embassy in Lebanon in 1985."(1)

Mario López de Miguel accurately details: "With the fall of the Palestine Liberation Organization (PLO) and the rise of Hezbollah, Israel was not simply exchanging one enemy for another. Hezbollah is recognized as one of the most significant terrorist groups in the world."(2)

The Spanish network SER describes the terrorist group as a real threat to the State of Israel and, even more importantly, as part of the Iranian regime, ""Hezbollah's military capacity has special relevance in the region due to the support and training it receives from Iran."

In fact, a report from the Spanish Institute for Strategic Studies (from Spain) considers this group directly an "integral part of the Iranian theocratic regime" that receives tens of thousands of missiles from Tehran.(3)

The terrorist attack on the Israeli embassy in Buenos Aires and the attack on the AMIA: the support of Iran and the action of Hezbollah

The terrorist attack on the Israeli embassy in Buenos Aires and the subsequent attack on the Argentine Israelite Mutual Association (AMIA), have left an indelible mark on the history of Argentina and on the Jewish people around the world. These acts of violence, perpetrated by the Hezbollah group, have been the subject of numerous investigations and debates over the years. Iran has provided support to Hezbollah in the planning and execution of these attacks, and there is much evidence to support this claim. However, the culprits have not yet been captured, despite having been identified years ago, both the intellectual perpetrators and those who carried out the attacks that cost the lives of 85 people, Jews and non-Jews.

Another important piece of evidence is the testimony of witnesses and collaborators who have revealed the connection between Iran and Hezbollah in relation to the attacks in Buenos Aires. These testimonies have been supported by international investigations and intelligence agencies, which have collected solid evidence linking Iran to the attacks.

Furthermore, it is important to highlight that the attacks in Buenos Aires are not isolated cases. Iran has been accused of supporting and financing terrorist groups around the world, and its relationship with Hezbollah is well known for this.

It is imperative that the international community continue to investigate and condemn these acts of terrorism, as well as the connections between Iran and Hezbollah, to ensure justice and prevent future attacks.

Hezbollah is a Shiite terrorist organization; whose goal is to establish an Islamic republic in Lebanon, eliminate Israel through armed conflict, combat American hegemony and savage capitalist forces (According to Hezbollah manifestos of 1985 and 2009). (4)

Composition and scope:

11

<u>General secretary:</u> Hassan Nasrallah

<u>Order of battle:</u> 45,000 (20,000 active duty soldiers and 25,000 reservists)

<u>Budget:</u> Hundreds of millions of dollars a year; They receive a large portion from Iran which supplies weapons, training, and intelligence, as well as financial support.

<u>Arsenal:</u> 120,000 - 130,000 missiles, including long-range missiles capable of reaching the entire State of Israel; sophisticated anti-tank weapons, dozens of unmanned aerial vehicles, advanced anti-ship missiles, advanced anti-aircraft missiles, and air security systems.

<u>Designation as a terrorist group:</u>

<u>The entire organization:</u> The Arab League, Argentina, Bahrain, Canada, Colombia, Germany, the Gulf Cooperation Council, Honduras, Israel, the Netherlands, Paraguay, the United Kingdom, and the United States.

<u>The military wing:</u> Australia, the European Union, and New Zealand.

<u>Participation in Syria:</u> Covert participation since 2012, public participation since 2013; active participation in major battles, including the Battle of Aleppo, the Battle of al-Qusayr, the Battle of Zabadani, the Siege of Homs, etc.

<u>Major terrorist attacks in the past:</u> Bus bombing in Burgas (6 victims, 2012), Khobar Towers bombing (19 victims, 1996), Flight 901 AC attack (21 victims, 1994), AMIA bombing in Argentina (85 deaths, 1994), Attack on the Israeli embassy in Buenos Aires (29 victims, 1992); 36 suicide attacks between 1982 and 1986, resulting in 659 deaths.

Chapter 6: Hamas-Isis, terror, torture, sadism and glorification of evil

History

Hamas is a branch that grew out of anti-Semitic Islamic movements.

˥ He broke away from the Muslim Brotherhood, a radical Islamist movement that was founded in Egypt in 1928 by a tough preacher named Hasan Al-Banna. Al-Banna was implacably opposed to the existence of a Jewish state.

˗ He admired Hitler and during World War II established posts of his movement in Jordan and what is now Israel. In 1948, he declared to The New York Times: "If the Jewish state becomes a fact... the Arab peoples... will throw the Jews living among them into the sea..." (6)

An influential representative of the Muslim Brotherhood was Ahmed Yassin, a popular preacher who spent most of his life in Gaza. He established a Palestinian branch of the Muslim Brotherhood in the 1970s and 1980s, and was arrested for creating a private army and collecting a huge amount of weapons. In 1987, he was one of the founders of Hamas.

Hamas was elected by popular vote

· There are two main Palestinian political parties: Fatah, which controls the Palestinian Authority and governs the West Strip, and Hamas, which governs Gaza.

Hamas was, incredibly, elected by the people. It seems unusual that he came to power through popular sovereignty.

· Two years after Israel's departure from Gaza, in 2007 Palestinians in the West Bank and Gaza held local elections. There, Hamas won a clear majority in both areas. The Fatah party ousted Hamas from government in the West Bank, but the terrorist group tightened its control over Gaza. There were never new elections in Gaza. Nor in the West Bank.

It is really difficult to understand that a violent group that advocates terror has managed to prevail at the polls. But let's remember that their "big brothers" who also wanted to eliminate Jews from the map, came to power by winning elections. Indeed, the Nazis prevailed in 1933 by winning the elections, making Adolf Hitler Chancellor of cultured and sophisticated Germany.

After what happened in the barbaric Hamas attack, it is possible to say without a doubt that the student turned out to be almost as sadistic and evil as his teacher.

Of course, with the gigantic difference that today, unlike the Nazi era, the State of Israel exists and its mission as a Jewish State is precisely to take charge of Judeophobic groups like Hamas-Isis.

Israel completely left Gaza in 2005

Israel conquered the West Bank from Jordan, and Gaza from Egypt during the Six-Day War in 1967, another confrontation that Israel did not initiate.

In 2005, under international pressure, Israel withdrew from Gaza, uprooting all Israelis and ensuring the area was completely free of Jews. Even Jewish graves were transferred.

The cowardly leadership of Hamas

Hamas leaders are protected, many of them are abroad.

The political head of Hamas is Ismail Hanieyeh, who lives in Doha, Qatar. Many senior Hamas leaders live with their families in Turkey, where they gained citizenship and run their own lucrative businesses. Muhamad Qassem Sawalha lives in a taxpayer-subsidized house in London, from where he helps plan terrorist attacks and launder money for Hamas.

Saleh al-Arouri heads the Hamas office in Lebanon, and lives there, but has homes in Qatar, Iran and Turkey. Khaled Mashal, the former leader of Hamas, lives in Qatar and recently called for a global jihad against the Jews. Khaled Qaddoumi is Hamas' representative in Iran, and Hamas' main backer in recent years.

High-level leaders living in Gaza include political leader Yahya Sinwar (who was imprisoned for 22 years in Israel for the arrest and murder of two Israeli soldiers). As well as Issam al-Daalis, who is the de facto prime minister of Gaza, and Marwan Issa and Mohammed Deif, who lead the Hamas military organization, and the Izz al Din al Qassam brigades.

Hamas is dedicated to the destruction of Israel

In Arabic, Hamas is an acronym for Hakarat al-Muqawama al-islamia, "Islamic resistance movement." (In Hebrew, Hamas means violence.) From the beginning, Hamas embodied both meanings, pledging to destroy Israel using all available means. Hamas' founding charter calls for the violent destruction of Israel and the creation of an Islamist state in its territory, Gaza and areas governed by the Palestinian Authority.

Hamas has carried out attacks against Israel since 1990

Hamas's military wing, called the Izz al-Din al-Qassam brigades, has attacked Israel incessantly since the 1990s. According to the US government: "These attacks have included large-scale bombings against Israeli civilian targets, attacks with small arms, improvised explosives on the roads and attacks with missiles." (5)

Hamas, today also called Hamas-Isis, is a Palestinian organization considered a terrorist group by many countries.

The history of Hamas and its impact on the region is a history of blood and violence, a vindication of terror. One of the methods most used by Hamas has been attacking buses. Over the years, they have carried out numerous suicide attacks in which they have detonated explosives on buses full of innocent civilians. These attacks have caused a large number of victims and have spread fear and insecurity among the population.

Launching missiles to kill civilians

Another method used by Hamas to sow terror is the launching of missiles into Israeli territory. These missiles, which are often launched from densely populated areas, endanger the lives of civilians in both Israel and Palestine.

In 2021, for example, Hamas launched more than 4,000 missiles at Israel, causing more than 300 victims and 10 deaths.

Hamas bombs Israel every day, and paradoxically, 20% of Hamas bombs fall in Gaza.

Hamas has been attacking Israel for years, launching mortars, rockets and incendiary devices into cities and towns in the country. Since October 7, 2023, Hamas has launched more than 8,500 thousand missiles, targeting important centers such as Jerusalem and Tel Aviv. Among the victims of these launches are the population that was in the Al-Ahri hospital, which was hit by a bomb launched by the Islamic Jihad group, on October 17, 2023, an attack for which Israel was first blamed.

.

Hamas' long history of terror has left a lasting impact on the region. It is imperative that the international community condemn these acts of violence and work together to find a peaceful and lasting solution to the conflict between Israel and Palestine. Only through a genuine recognition of the right of the Jewish State to exist and a true commitment of Palestinian diligence to renounce violence, will it be possible to move towards Peace in the Middle East.

Hamas murders and oppresses women, homosexuals and political opponents

Women's rights in Gaza are seriously compromised and they are banned from most government positions, forced to wear a black hijab in some public places, and face widespread state-sanctioned discrimination.

The Hamas statutes declare that Muslim women are important because they "make men." Amnesty International has documented that Hamas tolerates honor killings.

Of course, progressivism doesn't seem to care much about these "details."

Christian population persecuted by Hamas

Gaza's Christian population declined precipitously under Hamas rule to just a few hundred. The US government has documented "individual killings, physical attacks and verbal harassment of worshipers and clerics, vandalism at (Christian) religious sites in Hamas-ruled territory.

Probably, the mostly Christian Palestinian communities are not well aware of the situation, since otherwise it does not explain his markedly anti-Israeli behavior, when in the State of Israel Christians live in peace and are a substantive part of the Jewish State.

Hamas Financing

Hamas receives hundreds of millions of dollars in funding,

• Funds generated by Hamas: Hamas collects approximately $144 million a year in taxes on goods entering from Egypt. Also, it controls a vast secret network of companies with investments of 500 million dollars around the world. According to the United States Financial Crimes Enforcement Network, "Hamas moves funds through physical currency smuggling, as well as a regional network of complicit money transmitters, exchange houses, and Hezbollah-affiliated banks," allowing you to collect and reinvest money in most of the world with impunity.(7)

Donations: Hamas receives a huge amount of donations, at least $100 million a year from Iran, $360 million plus fuel from Qatar, and up to $300 million a year from Turkey, plus donations from and from charities around the world.

Theft of aid

• All of that is on top of the aid money flowing into Gaza, much of which is stolen directly by Hamas. The UN spends about $600 million annually in Gaza, providing schools, medical care and food. Qatar has donated around $1.3 billion in aid since 2012. The Palestinian Authority donates around $1.7 billion in aid each year. Other countries, including Egypt and the United States, as well as the European Union, also donate tens of millions of dollars for various aid projects. Most of that aid money doesn't go to poor civilians, but rather into the pockets of Hamas officials, and we already know where that money goes. The West remains undaunted by this reality. "There is no worse blind man than he who does not want to see."

Hamas invests in terror

Hamas built 500 km of terror tunnels, but no bomb shelters. It used the billions of dollars it received in aid to build a 500 km network of deep tunnels to move beneath Gaza, where barracks and war weapons have been installed, equipment that is moved through them and that extends towards Israel and Egypt. According to the Australian Political Strategy Institute, "The entrances to the Gaza tunnels are hidden beneath houses, mosques and schools...", densely populated places, turning the civilian population, especially children, into human shields, ensuring that any military attack causes multiple casualties.

The tunnels are up to three meters deep, reinforced with concrete and wired for ventilation, electricity and communications.

While Hamas leaders and fighters take refuge in the tunnels, this massive underground network is out of reach of ordinary Gazans. For Palestinian civilians used as human shields, there is no protection in times of war. Hamas did not build bomb shelters in Gaza. All of this has been profusely communicated to the world much of which seems to care.

Hamas: Anti-Jewish Definitions and Palestine without Jews

Hamas's political platform is based on armed resistance against the Israeli occupation and the creation of an independent Palestinian state. However, one of the main concerns regarding Hamas is its anti-Jewish rhetoric and its vision of a Palestine without Jews.

By spreading stereotypes and prejudices, Hamas contributes to polarization and hatred, rather than promoting dialogue and peaceful coexistence. This position is incompatible with the principles of equality and mutual respect that are fundamental to building a just and equitable society.

Furthermore, the vision of a Palestine without Jews goes against the values of diversity and pluralism. The history of Palestine is marked by the coexistence of different religious and ethnic communities.

Hamas's anti-Jewish rhetoric also negatively affects the perception of Palestine in the international community. By promoting exclusion and hatred of Jews, Hamas undermines efforts of solidarity and support for the Palestinian cause, as many human rights and justice advocates view these extremist positions with concern.

Hamas-Isis letter

The founding charter of Hamas-Isis is filled with paranoid rantings about Jews and calls for Muslims to kill them. "Israel, Judaism and Jews challenge Islam and the Muslim people," this document declares. He also quotes a Muslim command: "The day of judgment will not come until the Muslims fight the Jews. When the Jew hides behind stones and trees, the stones and trees will say: 'O Muslims... there is a Jew behind me. Come kill him.'" Without a doubt a delirious speech.

Some commentators point to a 2017 general principles and policies decree as "proof" that Hamas has become more moderate. In the midst of Arab-Israeli peace talks, the new Hamas-Isis document accepted the possibility of a two-state agreement with Israel, establishing an independent Palestinian state, but only as an intermediate step before the complete annihilation of Israel.

Indeed, the founding charter of Hamas-Isis calls for genocide, it is full of paranoid rantings about Jews and calls in the eyes of Hamas, Jews (and not just Israelis) are an enemy that must be eradicated. And not only the Jews, since for Hamas-Isis after Saturday comes Sunday, that is, after the Jews come the Christians.

As Ricardo Israel explains in Infobae "Perhaps they do not realize that, if Israel is defeated, medieval Islam is not going to be satisfied with this, but is going to try to reach a Europe that no longer fights to maintain its traditions, furthermore, it is not sustainable that they only want to cut off the heads of the Jews, but they also want to cut off the heads of other infidels, which includes those progressives in the streets of Europe and the USA (Australia or Argentina), whom they also hate, whatever they do marching in favor of Hamas. (72)

Article 6: Religious fundamentalism

The Islamic Resistance Movement is a Palestinian movement, which gives its loyalty to Allah, and whose way of life is Islam. Fight to raise the banner of Allah over every inch of Palestine [...]

Article 7: Example of anti-Semitism Islamic

[...] If the links have been distant from each other, and if obstacles placed in the path of the combatants by those who are lackeys of Zionism hampered the continuation of the struggle, the Islamic Resistance Movement aspires to the realization of the promise of Allah (destruction of the Jews), for as long as it takes. The Prophet, may Allah bless him and grant him salvation, has said: "The Day of Judgment will not come until the Muslims fight against the Jews (killing the Jews), when the Jew will hide behind stones and trees. The stones and the trees will say: Oh Muslims, oh Abdallah, there is a Jew behind me, come kill him. Only the gharkad tree (evidently a certain kind of tree) will not do it, because it is one of the trees of the Jews."

- Hamas anti-Semitism

Hamas's methods of infusing anti-Semitism vary. On the one hand we can see the symptoms of the stereotypes used by traditional European anti-Semitism (well known for having been used in Nazi propaganda).

A clear example is this video that deals with an alleged secret evil plan by the Jewish 'big noses' to destroy the Al-Aqsa mosque.

At other times, Hamas's anti-Semitism is based on a radical Islamic origin. For example, in the music video below, (made by Hamas's military wing, the Qassam Brigades) the part where it says *"killing the Jews is the task that brings us closer to Allah"* (0:34) is written behind a terrorist weapons depot.

- <u>Teaching hate</u>

The terrorist organization has gone to great lengths to indoctrinate Gaza's youth. This process begins with young children, through the television program "Sesame Street." Much has already been written about Hamas's own version of Mickey Mouse, Farfour, who was martyred by Israeli soldiers.

The words of Hamas leaders

Hamas leaders have constantly repeated the dogmatic and volatile speech of their letter. Ismail Haniyeh is Hamas's prime minister and leader inside the Gaza Strip.

He loves to give inflammatory speeches in which he repeatedly declares how he will never recognize Israel. Just like this big demonstration in Gaza in 2010, or the speech at the al-Azhar mosque in Cairo in March 2012.

Khaled Mashaal, Mashaal proclaimed: "Palestine is ours from the river to the sea and from the south to the north. There will be no concession on an inch of the land." (See again article 6 of the Charter).

Hamas was designated a terrorist organization

Hamas was designated as a terrorist organization by the United States, the European Union, (and 15 individual European Union member states), Canada, Great Britain, Australia and New Zealand.

The incredible influence of ISIS in the actions of Hamas' killing and torture

In recent years, the world has witnessed the growing influence of ISIS (Islamic State) in different conflicts and terrorist organizations around the world. One of the groups that has been impacted by this influence is Hamas, a Palestinian organization that has carried out numerous acts of violence in its fight against Israel.

First of all, it is important to highlight that ISIS has managed to establish an extremely effective communication and propaganda network. Through social networks and other media, they have managed to spread their radical and violent ideology, attracting followers and sympathizers around the world. Hamas, like other terrorist groups, has been influenced by this propaganda and has adopted tactics similar to those used by ISIS.

Second, ISIS's influence has manifested itself in Hamas's adoption of extremely brutal torture and execution methods. ISIS has been characterized by its cruelty and sadism, using methods such as beheading, crucifixion and public burning. These practices have been adopted by Hamas, which has carried out summary executions and inhumane torture against those it considers traitors or collaborators with Israel.

Furthermore, ISIS's influence has extended to Hamas's military strategy; ISIS has proven to be a highly organized and disciplined group, capable of carrying out coordinated and sophisticated attacks. Hamas has adopted these tactics, carrying out surprise attacks and using more advanced weaponry. This has led to an increase in the effectiveness of their operations and a higher number of victims.

On the other hand, the influence of ISIS has also manifested itself in the radicalization of Hamas members. ISIS has managed to attract disaffected and marginalized youth, offering them a sense of belonging and purpose through its extremist ideology. Hamas has experienced a similar phenomenon, recruiting young Palestinians who feel frustrated and hopeless about the situation in the region. These young people are easily influenced and are willing to carry out acts of violence in the name of the cause.

In short, the influence of ISIS in the actions of Hamas' killing and torture is undeniable. Through its propaganda and brutal tactics, ISIS has managed to influence the military strategy and ideology of Hamas. This has led to an increase in the violence and cruelty of the actions perpetrated by this Palestinian terrorist group. It is essential that the international community continues to combat the influence of ISIS and work to find peaceful solutions to conflicts in the region.

Hamas is admired in much of the Muslim world

After Hamas' horrific and brutal attacks on Israel on October 7, 2023, in which more than 1,400 people were brutally murdered and more than 240 kidnapped, leaders across much of the Muslim world praised Hamas' attacks. The leaders of Iraq, Syria, Iran and Lebanon praised Hamas for the attacks. In the West, some groups (including individuals, social democratic groups in the United States and Black Lives Matter) spoke positively of the Hamas attacks. Leaders of a recent 100,000-person pro-Palestinian march in central London shouted slogans in favor of the Hamas terrorist group. And to this day the president of the Palestinian Authority has not clearly condom the atrocious the barbarity carried out by the Hamas-Isis terrorist group.

Chapter 7: The horror and barbarism of October

The holiday of Simchat Torah should have been a day of joy for Israel and the Jewish people. That Saturday was a Shabbat supposedly of rest and entertainment. But everything was stained with blood and pain. The October war will remain engraved in the collective memory of a country that mourns its dead and that will take a long time to return to "normality." This war in particular, which was already characterized by the horror and barbarity that was unleashed mercilessly against Israel and the Jewish people, also generating a wave of anti-Semitism and Judeophobia unprecedented in recent decades.

Horror and barbarism are terms that conjure images of extreme violence, destruction and suffering. Unfortunately, Israel was the victim of a series of acts that fit this description perfectly. It was a day when peace and tranquility were overshadowed by violence and chaos.

The barbaric acts of Hamas-Isis rape women and girls, murder of children, burning babies alive, kidnappings, parading Israeli women as trophies through the streets of Gaza, torturing children in front of their parents, mutilating bodies in that there are many who cannot be identified and an endless series of sadism and evil aimed at causing as much harm and pain as possible.

CNN, a medium that is characterized by its marked editorial line that is always critical of the Jewish State, reported what "Hamas attackers[1] They killed babies in front of their parents and then murdered them" (58)

Testimonies of the Hamas massacre

The extremist group Hamas has been accused of carrying out numerous acts of violence, including the killing of civilians. The testimonies of the massacre perpetrated by Hamas are extremely painful and terrible.

Hamas, an organization considered terrorist by many countries, has been accused of carrying out indiscriminate attacks against Israeli civilians. These acts of violence have left a trail of death and destruction in the region, and have generated a military response from Israel.

Hamas usually fired rockets trying to kill Jews and then, as Professor Ricardo Israel explains, continued using methods that contravene the conventions regulating war. Professor Israel states: "According to international law, it is not about quantity, which is also the reason why the use of human shields is punished, which seeks to increase the number of deaths to influence emotionality through propaganda and social media effects."(8)

The Hamas-Isis terrorist group had us "accustomed" to these terrorist activities, but we had never seen the level of evil, sadism and perversion that dominated the terrorist actions on the day that Israel should have been celebrating the giving of the Torah, the five books of the Bible (Genesis, Exodus, Leviticus, Numbers and Deuteronomy) to the Jewish people. There was no celebration, no dancing, or anything like that. Israel cried with grief and rage while young people, children, adults, babies and the elderly were tortured and massacred mercilessly in 22 places near the border with Gaza.

Some of the most shocking testimonies of the survivors of the attacks perpetrated by Hamas, by those who managed to survive the storm of ruthless evil and sadism, gave an account of the horror and hell that had been experienced in the south of Israel. These people tell how they witnessed indiscriminate violence, which does not distinguish between men, women or children. These testimonies are essential to understand the magnitude of the acts committed by Hamas and the need to take measures to prevent future massacres by this heartless terrorist group.

---

1. https://cnnespanol.cnn.com/2023/10/11/ultima-hora-conflicto-israel-gaza-vivo-hamas-orix/

In addition to the testimonies of survivors, there is also documentary evidence that supports the accusations against Hamas. Images and videos captured during the attacks clearly show the violence and destruction caused by this extremist group. This evidence is essential to establish Hamas' responsibility for the massacre and to demand justice for the victims.

Hamas-Isis calls their terrifying actions a legitimate response to the Israeli occupation and the oppressive policies they have carried out.

They argue that their goal is to resist and liberate Palestine from the occupation and of course rid it of all the Jews. These statements have no validity whatsoever, they are painfully insubstantial and largely false and absurd and in no case do they justify indiscriminate terrorist violence, much less the killing of innocent civilians.

Like any terrorist movement, it is based on lies and deception to achieve its nefarious and horrific objectives.

The testimonies of the massacre perpetrated by Hamas are clear evidence of the violence and brutality of this extremist group. Survivors and documentary evidence support the accusations against Hamas and demonstrate the need to take measures to prevent future acts of violence. Although Hamas argues that its actions are a legitimate response, the killing of innocent civilians cannot be justified. It is essential that the international community abandon its well-known anti-Israeli behavior and truly and without nuance or context condemn these horrible acts and truly work together with the only democracy in the Middle East to find a just, peaceful and lasting solution to the conflict between Israel and Palestine. To do this, we will have to find some Palestinian group that truly believes in the legitimate right of the Jewish people to have a state and to live in secure borders.

In the history of humanity, we have witnessed numerous acts of barbarism that have left a deep scar on our collective conscience. However, few events have been as heinous and merciless as the acts committed by Hamas-Isis that fateful Saturday. The barbarity of the acts perpetrated by Hamas shows that it is an extremist organization that rapes women and girls, murders children and burns babies alive.

On October 7, we witnessed the largest pogrom in history, after the extermination camps of the Nazi regime were closed.

The Hamas-Isis terrorist group managed to enter Israel, tortured and murdered women, children, men, older adults and also many of their pets, whose sin was living with Jews. Now we know very well what the cry means in English: "Free Palestine from the river to the sea".

The leaders of this horrific and sadistic organization have vowed to return to torturing Jews until there are none left in what they define as Palestine, in their words annihilating Israel. "A senior Hamas official openly committed to perpetuating terrorist acts against Israel, ensuring that he will continue these attacks "over and over again" until the complete annihilation of the country, ratifying the October 7 attack."(71)

Hamas does not respect the conventions that regulate wars

Professor Ricardo Israel explains in Infobae that, contrary to what is believed, the Hamas-Isis terrorist group is also subject to the regulations and regulations of wars.

"The purpose of war is the subjugation of the enemy, so the choice of means and methods should not have as its primary objective the death of civilians. On the contrary, every just war is understood as the defense of human beings, which is why it seeks to punish if the main objective of the war activity is harm to the civilian population, especially if this exceeds the military advantage that the attack provides, that is, the opposite of what happened on October 7, where its main objective was to attack civilians, usually the purpose of any terrorist action."(8).

It also violates all agreements and conventions in the mistreatment and possible torture of prisoners of war. (18)

Result of the massacre of Jews by the Hamas-Isis terrorist group

So far, the result of the massacre is, among others; 21 children from 13 families without parents after the Hamas attack; one is a 4 year old hostage.

The Ministry of Social Welfare's figure includes 16 cases in which both parents were killed by terrorists; For the remaining children, one of their parents was murdered, while the other was kidnapped or is missing.

Acts of rape against women and girls are one of the cruelest forms of gender violence. In the case of Hamas-Isis, the violations were carried out with unimaginable brutality. The victims, many of them minors, were subjected to unbearable physical and psychological suffering. These acts not only violated the integrity of the victims, but also left profound consequences on the mental and emotional health of those who survived.

The barbaric acts committed by Hamas on October 7 have left an indelible mark on human history. The rape of women and girls, the murder of children and the burning of babies alive are acts that defy any sense of humanity and compassion. Another aspect that stands out in this event is the lack of empathy and compassion on the part of the perpetrators. Violence and barbarism were not only manifested in physical acts, but also in the way they were carried out. Cruelty and indifference towards the suffering of others are characteristics that cannot be tolerated in a civilized society. That is why it is so shocking and frightening to see demonstrations in favor of Hamas.

It is urgent to review the educational content that Palestinian children have and eliminate each and every reference to anti-Semitism and Judeophobia.

Islamic fundamentalist terrorism seeks to install Shaharia in Israel first and in the world later. Although many do not want to see it, what they express is "first on Saturday and then on Sunday" that is, first the Jews and then the Christians.

We had a brutal synopsis of what would happen the day Israel loses a war, the torture, murders, kidnappings, rapes and sadism taken to its maximum expression, burning babies or cutting their throats.

Not since the doors of Auschwitz were closed has there been such a terrible day for the Jews, and I am sure for much of the world. More than 1,400 murdered, thousands injured and more than 200 Israelis kidnapped, including 30 children under 12 years old and some Holocaust survivors.

The victims are mostly families from the kibbutzim near the border and young people who ironically were at "a party for peace," which makes everything even more painful.

The Palestinian terrorists were in charge of showing the world the rapes, kidnappings, murders and torture, they were the ones who uploaded photos and videos of the horrific actions they carried out for hours, where they went house to house raping, robbing and killing.

Once it became known in the Gaza Strip that people could enter to rob, rape, kill and loot, an unknown number of Palestinian families joined this true festival of blood and exaltation of evil.

Although it may be difficult to believe, among those families who came in unleashed to cause the greatest pain possible, there were many who were or were rather employees of the kibbutzim.

Testimonies of horror

Supernova: the festival of death

Party Held in a forested area of Re'i'm where Hamas murdered more than 260 people, it was the cruel scene of the massacre where they were celebrating a festival for peace.

"La Vanguardia" reported: "The music stopped suddenly. We thought there was some electrical problem, but suddenly we started hearing like a bombardment. At first we thought it was a sound coming from the speakers. It was half past six "(9)

Journalist Carles Villalonga reports "At dawn on Saturday,while some 3,000 young Israelis danced to the rhythm of music[2] **electronics at a festival in the desert,**Hamas militiamen[3] **Arriving from Gaza, they burst in armed to the teeth,**They massacred 260 people[4] **and**They kidnapped several more[5]**, in which it is the bloodiest episode of this new war."** (eleven)

Niv Cohen, survivor: "Around 6:30 in the morning on Saturday, with the first rays of the sun, the anti-aircraft alarms and the sound of rockets launched from Gaza forced the festival music to stop." Cohen, one of those who were able to survive the massacre, says that the first indication they received when they saw the Hamas guerrillas was "to lie down on the ground, because that is the procedure: stretch out, put your hands on your head and wait." ten minutes". (10) "We tried to leave the party area, but we understood that many terrorists had come to massacre us," Gal Raz, a 31-year-old Israeli, told Efe from his home on the outskirts of Tel Aviv.(11)

While some stayed hidden, others, like Cohen and his friends, felt another impulse, which led them to react: "La Vanguardia" collected the testimony "I felt that we had to do something more. That's why we ran away. Those who remained on the ground have ended up either shot dead or kidnapped."(10)

That's when they realized that terrorists were on the ground. "They came down from the sky on paragliders, but they also arrived with cars and motorcycles. And they shot at everything. Against the people who were fleeing, against the cars.

Even when we managed to flee and left the parking lot and entered the road, we saw dead people on the sides of the road and we were aware that we were in a war zone" reported "La Vanguardia".(10)

"We saw many destroyed cars and bodies everywhere. We have not found our friends, we believe they are all dead or kidnapped." (12)

Luckily, they managed to escape: "It was a second, just a second before everything happened. We saw them shooting at people who were driving. We managed to escape successfully, but we saw many people leaving the car and running away."(12)

Others had much more trouble fleeing. Raz, who with the first rockets and the sound of gunshots separated from the friend he had come with, then decided to escape towards the south with another group of Israelis, but a few meters

2. https://www.lavanguardia.com/internacional/20231008/9285378/shani-louk-israel-gaza-turista-alemana-ataque-video.amp.html

3. https://www.lavanguardia.com/internacional/20231008/9285152/israel-guerra-hamas.amp.html

4. https://www.lavanguardia.com/internacional/20231008/9285830/hallados-260-cuerpos-desierto-celebraban-festival-asalto-hamas.amp.html

5. https://www.lavanguardia.com/internacional/20231010/9288773/israel-ordena-asedio-total-gaza.amp.html

away they encountered an ambush by Palestinian militiamen who opened fire on him. vehicle in which they were traveling. (eleven)

Shani Louk, the German victim of the Hamas attack exposed in an atrocious video[6] She was paraded around as a trophy like many other girls and women who were cruelly raped and tortured.(13))

"We managed to escape, but the car stopped and we had to continue on foot." Their plan then was to run to the nearest community, six kilometers away, but their relatives informed them that Hamas had taken control of several nearby towns and suggested they hide in the brush.(11)

Raz remained with four people, lying down and with his head next to the ground, watching militiamen pass by a few meters from where he was, during the eight hours it took for the army to arrive.

It was at that moment when he was able to watch a video on his cell phone in which he saw his friend, Avinatán Or, being kidnapped and taken to Gaza with his girlfriend, Noa Argamani, images that quickly went viral on social networks.

"They took mothers, pregnant women, children, elderly people. "They only came to cause panic and disaster."

Gal Raz, a survivor, has since lived with sadness, despair and fury. While he expresses frustration at the slow reaction of Israeli security forces, his anger is directed at the Palestinian militias: "After what they did on Saturday, Hamas and Palestinian Islamic Jihad must cease to exist."(11)

"They not only took Avinatán and Noa, they took mothers, pregnant women, children, elderly people. They only came to cause panic and disaster to our people," concludes Raz, who has joined a campaign to press for the release of adults, children and babies kidnapped by the Hamas-Isis terrorist group.

Among the countless number of Israelis who have been searching since Saturday for their loved ones without receiving a response, is Daizy Moshe, whose younger brother, Oz Moshe, has not shown any signs of life since he tried to escape from the same festival.

That morning, the 24-year-old young man communicated with his brother by video call while fleeing the attack after having been shot three times: one in the leg, one in the chest and one in the back.

"We were in contact for about 15 minutes, we could hear the gunshots and explosions in the background and Noemí, his girlfriend, was talking to the emergency services so they could tell her how to help him," Daizy narrates in dialogue with Efe.

"At one point he told me that they had shot the girl who was driving and then I began to hear desperate screams, followed by a wave of gunshots. Then it was all silence. I was on the call for 10 minutes, in silence," he says in a broken voice, having just arrived from the funeral of Noemí, whose body was identified yesterday by a DNA sample.

"Mediatiko.com" published: "One of the survivors detailed how he was able to escape from that place, fleeing the bullets and hiding in a small concrete shelter. "The terrorists threw a grenade inside, which exploded into pieces. There was blood everywhere," he confessed, in the middle of crying.(15)

The journalist Daniel Molio on "radio Jai" emphasized something very painful and perhaps one of the most relevant issues regarding the identification of the bodies: "1,000 corpses have been identified, not only do the other 400 still need to be identified, but perhaps many cannot be identified because they have been cremated."(16)

---

6. https://www.lavanguardia.com/internacional/20231008/9285378/shani-louk-israel-gaza-turista-alemana-ataque-video.amp.html

Chapter 8: Killing and torture in the kibbutzim

The kibbutzim are the most successful socialist experience in history. Initially, they were conceived as socialist collective farms, where it was shared under a regime of equality. Each person gave what they could and received what they needed.

Before the creation of the state of Israel, this progressive experiment was also very useful to cultivate the land and protect itself from the constant attacks of the Arabs, who for centuries have viewed infidels who do not profess Islam with suspicion.

There is hardly any other organization created and that has lasted as effective and as efficient as the kibbutzim. The truth is that ironically the radical left that so indiscriminately criticizes the Jewish State would do well to try to learn from the success of the kibbutzim to this day. .

Hamas torture

US Secretary of State Antony Blinken recalls scenes of the atrocious massacre perpetrated by Hamas on 7/10. What he says is difficult to hear: "The father's eye was gouged out in front of his children, the mother's breast was cut off, the girl's foot was amputated, the boy's fingers were cut off, before being executed. And then his executioners sat down to eat."(53)

The victims of the kibbutzim

The testimony of Dalia Fishman, an Israeli citizen living in Tel Aviv, reveals the atrocities committed by the terrorist group Hamas towards the Israeli population during the conflict in Israel and Palestine. Fishman reports the disappearance of five members of his family, including his twin sister, his brother-in-law, his nieces and his brother-in-law's brother, following the Hamas attack. The last news he had of his family was on Saturday before ten in the morning, when Dalia sent him a message asking if he was okay and he never answered her again.(17)

At a kibbutz near Gaza, soldiers found up to 40 dead babies, many of them decapitated, and entire families shot to death in their beds. Fishman says that his soldier nephew received WhatsApp messages from his family saying that terrorists were in their house and were trying to break into the shelter. His 22-year-old niece called her brother on the phone and all she heard were screams of horror, strange noises and men speaking in Arabic, indicating the presence of Hamas terrorists.

At the moment, it is unknown if his family members are prisoners or murdered. In the kibbutz, where around 1,200 people live, at least 100 are estimated to be dead. Most of the bodies have been destroyed by the terrorists, making reconnaissance difficult.

Dalia Fishman denounces these acts as a war crime and asks for the intervention of different countries to stop these atrocities, which she describes as a "Holocaust." His last wish is to know the whereabouts of his family, although he prefers them to be dead rather than continue suffering as prisoners.

Her twin sister, who had a leftist ideology and believed in reconciliation between Israelis and Palestinians, lost all hope during the Hamas attack. Dalia also shared that opinion, but now sees the situation with different eyes and criticizes that "they don't want a country," referring to the Hamas terrorists.

Dalia Fishman's testimony shows the suffering and anguish experienced by families affected by the conflict in Israel and Palestine.

Mayaan Levi still has a hard time remembering how he had to seek refuge with his neighbors in Ofakim and remain silent, for fear of being discovered by Hamas fighters. "We were afraid to make any sound (...) basically we were afraid to even breathe," he told the "Voice of America.""

Like hundreds of Israelis, Levi's reality changed on Saturday, October 7, when the Islamic militant group stormed into territory near the Gaza Strip. Ofakim, about 18 kilometers from the area controlled by Hamas, is among the furthest points reached by the extremists.(18)

"There were shootings, we didn't know what was happening, the neighbors were leaving [...] some neighbors went and fought for us, they took weapons and protected us," says the young woman while showing the bullet holes in the walls of her house, now covered with a large flag of Israel.

Yoni Asher says he recognized his wife Doron, and his daughters Aviv and Raz as they were being loaded onto a truck by militants.

Some families are testifying to the panic they feel after learning that their relatives have been kidnapped by Hamas, during the Palestinian terrorist group's attack on Israel.

The newspaper La Vanguardia" reported in detail on the massacre perpetrated by Hamas-Isis in southern Israel: "After not receiving information about his brother, Daizy traveled with the rest of his family to the festival site to try to find him."(9)

"We didn't find his car, his body, anything. We saw many destroyed cars and bodies everywhere. We have not found his friends either, we believe they are all dead or kidnapped, but the only information we receive is what we see on television." (9)

Dozens of bodies have been found, entire families, including women and children. In chilling testimonies, journalists and witnesses to what happened reported that they found themselves the bodies of 40 murdered babies, some of them decapitated while they slept.

Along the same lines, a member of the Israeli army's health teams assured that he himself "found a baby with its head cut off" among the more than 100 people murdered in the Beeri kibbutz, next to the Strip.

Members of his team found more decapitated children, added reserve Colonel Golan Vach, head of the National Rescue Unit in the Army's Internal Front Command. In his opinion, "terrorism means that a person enters the home of innocent people, kills the mother and cuts off the baby's head."

A member of the ZAKA emergency teams, which is in charge of recovering bodies, told EFE that "he does not have numbers, but that there are many cases" of dead children in places like Be'eri.

The newspaper "El Clarín", citing a BBC report, tells about the barbarity of the commandos of the HAMAS group during the bloody October 7 assault:[1] "Bodies continue to be found, many of them children, with significant signs of torture, the chain indicates." (14)

"Even the most experienced health workers are being challenged by what they see, deaths like these are enough to break the living," journalist Lucy Williams points out in that work from Nir Oz, near the Strip.(20)

One of the bodies found in Kibbutz Be'eri was that of a woman. "She was naked and her feet were tied with barbed wire." One of the team members said that "corpses of more than 20 children had been found, tied and burned."(21)

Videos recorded by the terrorists themselves, Infobae reported: "Other images show a group of Israelis who were taken to the Strip. There they are received by Hamas militants who kick and hit them, while shouting "Allah is Great." Near those hostages, on the side of the street, a handful of dead people lie next to some parked cars."(21)

Now, videos show murdered babies, children inside forensic bags with their identification, and a kibbutz house with a huge trail of spilled blood.

When that video cuts, a dozen corpses appear inside a gazebo. And then, a road with abandoned cars that exhibit - again - the brutality of the terrorists: inside there are dead people with their eyes open and in the fetal position.

At minute 35, footage shows Israelis being killed and then set on fire. There are charred bodies of all ages, which have not yet been identified. They are anonymous dead.

---

1.   https://www.clarin.com/mundo/israel-guerra-masivo-ataque-sorpresa-hamas-gaza_0_Vy2ejHPkNo.html

The video fades to black and audio appears in Arabic: the terrorists are heard talking to their parents, who are in the Gaza Strip.

"Mom I killed ten Jews, I killed them with my hands. Allah is powerful, mom. "I killed ten Jews" is heard. ( )

"Where are you?" -answers the mother-. "Return safe and sound."(64)

"Yes mom. I killed ten Jews. I killed ten Jews. Look at my WhatsApp. Look at my WhatsApp"(21)

Major General Michael Edelstein spent many years fighting in the Gaza Strip, and was in charge of explaining to "Infobae" and other journalists why they made the 43-minute video showing the massacre committed by Hamas. Edelstein, a tough and long-experienced general, confessed without flinching:"I never saw anything like this".

"Digital Freedom" reported: "The Israeli soldiers are entering the homes that were attacked, some of them also set on fire. They are finding dozens of bodies, entire families, including women and children.

In a chilling testimony, journalists who witnessed the work explain that they have found the bodies of 40 murdered babies, some of them decapitated while they slept."(22)

Chapter 9: The immense and devastating pain of Israel: 1,400 dead, thousands injured and 240 kidnapped, including children

In recent days, Israel has witnessed a series of tragic events that have left deep pain in its society. With 1,400 dead, thousands injured and 240 kidnapped, including innocent children, it is evident that suffering in Israel is a reality that cannot be ignored. This argumentative essay will analyze the causes and consequences of this pain, as well as possible solutions to alleviate it.

Causes of pain in Israel

The pain in Israel is rooted in the horrific action of Hamas-Isis terrorism.

Arab tensions and attacks have led to a series of violent clashes, terrorist attacks and military reprisals. These events have left a trail of death and destruction, generating deep pain in Israeli society.

Furthermore, the kidnapping of people, including children, has further aggravated the suffering in Israel. These inhuman acts have left emotional and psychological scars on the victims and their families, generating pain that lasts over time.

The pain in Israel has had a significant impact on society and the daily lives of its inhabitants. The families of the victims have experienced irreparable loss, while the injured have faced long-term physical and emotional difficulties.

Furthermore, the kidnapping of people has generated a climate of fear and mistrust in Israeli society, affecting the quality of life of all its citizens.

To alleviate the pain in Israel, it is essential that the Jewish state be able to defend itself.

Only through a strong and secure Israel will peace in the region be ensured and a lasting solution eventually reached.

Finally, it is essential that the international community plays an active, balanced and impartial role in the search for a peaceful solution. The mediation and support of international organizations can only be effective if they abandon their brutal, markedly anti-Israeli actions. Only then can they achieve the legitimacy that they lack today and thus eventually help generate a climate conducive to seeking a peace that must certainly be contemplated. the security of the Jewish State.

The pain in Israel, with its 1,400 dead, thousands injured and 240 kidnapped, including innocent children, is a reality that cannot be ignored. It is essential that dialogue be promoted, support provided to victims and international intervention sought to ensure the right of the state of Israel to defend itself from terrorism.

Only in this way can the pain be partially overcome and a future of peace and prosperity built for all the inhabitants of Israel.

The world's response has been one of impact and solidarity, probably because images were devastating and undeniable.

Chapter 10: World's response to the Hamas massacre: Israel must defend itself

In recent years, we have witnessed numerous acts of violence perpetrated by Hamas, a terrorist organization that seeks the destruction of the State of Israel. In response to these attacks, Israel has taken measures to defend itself and protect its population. However, the world's response to the Hamas massacre has been largely unbalanced and biased.

It is urgent to recognize the need to recognize Israel's right to defend itself.

Importantly, Israel has the right and responsibility to protect its population from terrorist attacks. Hamas has launched thousands of rockets into Israeli cities, endangering the lives of innocent civilians. These indiscriminate attacks not only violate international law, but also undermine any chance for peace in the region. In this sense, Israel has carried out military operations to neutralize threats and guarantee the security of its population.

The reasons why Israel has the right to defend itself

Israel has every right to defend itself against its enemies who seek to wipe it off the map. Carmelo Jorda, journalist for Libertad Digital and esRadio, offers a concise summary of the 7 reasons why Israel has the right to defend itself.

Jorda effectively lays out the political and legal reasons why Israel can and should defend its citizens.(24)

1. Continued Hamas rocket attacks: Since Israel's withdrawal from Gaza in 2005, Hamas has launched thousands of rockets targeting Israeli civilians, causing significant property damage and generating fear among the Israeli population.

2. Hamas's goal of destruction: Hamas, as a recognized terrorist organization, is explicitly committed to the destruction of Israel. You cannot reach peace agreements with an organization whose objective is to destroy your country. Additionally, Hamas employs tactics such as indiscriminate rocket attacks on Israeli civilians, demonstrating its disregard for human life.

3. Israel does not occupy Gaza: Israel completely withdrew from Gaza in 2005, dismantling all military installations and settlements in the area. Gaza is not an occupied territory, although Israel exercises control over its borders to prevent new arming by Hamas. Additionally, Israel allows tons of food, fuel, medicine and construction materials to pass into Gaza through open border crossings.

4. No rewards for killers: Unlike Hamas, which rewards Palestinian terrorists with financial support, Israel aggressively pursues and prosecutes Israeli terrorists who harm Palestinians. Israeli society, as well as political and religious leaders, condemn the acts of violence.

5. International law supports Israel's right to self-defense: Every sovereign State has the right to defend itself against unlawful aggression and take measures to prevent future attacks. Israel's military operations in Gaza are framed within the right to self-defense recognized by international law.

6. Israel's will for peace: Israel has repeatedly demonstrated its readiness for peace, while Hamas has repeatedly violated ceasefires and launched rockets in response to Israeli military interventions.

This illustrates Hamas's lack of interest in peace and its commitment to continue attacking Israel.

7. Israel as an initial defense against Islamist extremism: Israel is the first line of defense for the Western world against Islamist extremism. Islamist terrorists consider Spain as a Muslim land that must be reconquered. In fighting the same enemy that threatens Western civilization, Israel plays a crucial role.

Israel undoubtedly possesses the right to defend itself from Hamas terrorist attacks. With Hamas' continued rocket fire, its goal of destruction, Israel's lack of occupation of Gaza, the difference in responses to terrorism, the support of international law, Israel's pursuit of peace and its role as the Western world's leading defender against Islamist extremism, it is essential to support Israel in its fight against terrorism and its search for peace.

However, the world's response to the Hamas massacre has been largely disproportionate and biased. Many countries and international organizations have condemned Israel without taking into account the context in which this conflict takes place. It is essential to understand that Israel does not seek violence, but is forced to defend itself against terrorist attacks. The international community should recognize this fact and support Israel's efforts to protect its population.

Furthermore, it is important to note that Hamas uses cynical and despicable tactics by hiding behind the civilian population. They use schools, hospitals and mosques, endangering the lives of their own citizens. This perverse strategy makes it even more difficult for Israel to conduct precise military operations and minimize civilian casualties. However, the international community seems to ignore this aspect and focuses only on civilian casualties, without taking into account the responsibility of Hamas in this situation.

On the other hand, it is important to mention that Israel has demonstrated its willingness to seek peaceful and negotiated solutions. It has participated in numerous peace attempts and has shown its willingness to compromise for the sake of regional stability. However, Hamas has consistently rejected any attempt at dialogue and has opted for violence as a means to achieve its goals. This stubborn and belligerent attitude of Hamas not only harms the Palestinian population, but also hinders any possibility of reaching a peaceful and lasting solution.

In conclusion, the world's response to the Hamas massacre has been unbalanced and biased. Israel has the right and responsibility to defend itself from terrorist attacks carried out by Hamas. The international community should recognize this fact and support Israel's efforts to protect its population.

Chapter 11: The wave of anti-Semitism

History repeats itself over and over again, every time the Jewish State defends itself from constant terrorist attacks, such as the Hamas bombings in Israeli cities for 15 years, a good part of the world automatically reacts against Israel and of course against the Jews all over the planet.

Following these attacks, accusations of disproportionate use of force by the Jewish State arise, which in turn gives rise to a wave of anti-Semitic and Judeophobic demonstrations. However, this time there is a notable difference, as Alejo Schapire highlights: "The great news is that the wave of anti-Semitism began with the Hamas attack, even before Israel fired a single shot."

It is true that anti-Semitism is a symptom of a deeper problem: fanaticism and intolerance, as Daniel Pipes affirms, but certainly this destructive anti-Semitic contamination has no comparison with what was experienced in other wars of the Jewish State.

In places like the Paris metro, groups of young people, often of Muslim origin, shout insults against Jews and declare themselves proud to be Nazis. A Muslim cleric has also been arrested in southern Paris for calling for the murder of Jews, and Stars of David have been painted on walls in Paris and many cities around the world. The intensity and force with which this anti-Semitic storm has hit places like New York is a new phenomenon, since the United States had always been considered a safe haven for the Jewish community.

Several factors influence this anti-Semitic sentiment, but according to Schapire, two stand out. The first factor is the type of immigration that has been established in the United States in recent years, which embraces anti-Semitism as part of its Muslim identity, seeing Israel as an unjust occupation and the Palestinian cause as something that unites all people. Arabs and Muslims in their hatred of Israel. As Schapire mentions: "Anti-Semitism has become part of their Muslim identity and is instilled in their home and place of origin, transmitted by clerical leaders and educators."

"We must seek truth and justice instead of perpetuating stereotypes and prejudices." But without a doubt the response to the barbarism and sadism of Hamas-Isis has been devastating and disappointing, not only confirming what the French intellectual affirms but making even more painful the tremendous wound of that black Shabbat of October.

The second factor that Schapire highlights is progressivism, which presents the Palestinian people as "the noble savage", innocent by definition, and has reversed historical roles, turning the Jew into the new Nazi. According to Schapire: "The Israeli-Palestinian conflict has become a battlefield of ideological and political concepts, where the essential thing is a narrative of oppressor and oppressed, with the Palestinian people always being the oppressed and the just."

This deep-rooted anti-Semitic sentiment is partly due to historical movements, such as the paradigm shift following the Holocaust. Before World War II, the Jew was considered the "other," a parasite that threatened the racial purity of Europe. However, as awareness of the Holocaust grew and independence movements emerged in the former colonies, the focus shifted to the "other" and everything that was not the "Aryan man." The Jews, by establishing their own state, became the colonizers and were seen as the polar opposite of the United States, denounced as imperialist and capitalist.

In Europe and Latin America, the radical left plays an important role in supporting Hamas. The radical left has focused its attention on culture, especially ethnic and sexual minorities, and has adopted concepts such as intersectionality, which maintains that all oppressed minorities must unite to confront the Western heterosexual white man, presented as the ultimate enemy. However, this theory ignores the reality of the situation and the inherent contradiction of defending a repressive organization like Hamas, as exemplified by the irony of LGBTQ+ people supporting a group that would likely harm or even kill them if they were in the Gaza Strip for just five minutes.

Additionally, philosopher Slavoj Žižek criticizes the current trend of blaming Israel and Jews for all the world's ills, using language and ideologies that seem progressive but actually perpetuate old anti-Semitic stereotypes and prejudices.

Žižek argues that by focusing solely on Israel, attention is diverted from other problems and political actors that also bear responsibility for the region's conflicts.

Regarding Latin America's support for Hamas, Schapire highlights that although the actors may change, the discourse remains the same. Interestingly, these anti-Semitic attacks end up legitimizing the Zionist project, reaffirming the need for armed protection for Jews around the world, including in places like New York. The resurgence of anti-Semitism disguised as anti-racism portrays Jews as the new Nazis and Palestinians as the new Jews, perpetuating a sinister historical inversion where any action taken by Palestinians is explainable and justifiable, while any action taken by Israelis is condemned. , regardless of their actions.

In conclusion, the wave of anti-Semitism arising in response to Israel's attacks on Hamas is a worrying and unfortunately common phenomenon. It is based on a number of factors, such as Muslim immigration that embraces anti-Semitism as part of their identity, progressivism that reverses historical roles and presents Israel as the oppressor and Palestinians as the innocent victims, and support from the left. radical that is based on concepts such as intersectionality. This wave of hatred and discrimination must be addressed vigorously and work must be done to promote education, dialogue and mutual respect between different cultural and religious groups, to combat anti-Semitism and build more inclusive and tolerant societies.

Anti Semitism is not simply a problem for the Jewish community, but has dire consequences for all those committed to the universal values of freedom, equality and tolerance.

Likewise, combating anti-Semitism requires solid education, a firm denunciation of hate speech and a constant defense of the human rights and dignity of all people, clearly and without buts denouncing the savage terrorism of Hamas-Isis, Herzbollah and all groups led by the tyrannical regime of Iran

Chapter 12: The sad and painful response of the left to the Hamas massacre

The truth is that it is unusual and incredible that there are people in their right mind who consider that carrying out all these aberrations can be called "resistance", it is difficult to understand so much evil, myopia, fanaticism or simply anti-Semitism.

The world on the left is blind and deaf when it comes to Israel. There seems to be an autopilot that dictates that Israel is guilty of all the evils in the Middle East conflict. It is a shame and a shame to see how people indirectly support Hamas without taking into account the reality of the situation. This generates deep anger and frustration.

The left, in its desire to defend the oppressed, has adopted an unwavering stance against Israel. However, this position is based on a distorted view of the facts and a lack of understanding of the complexity of the situation in the region.

It is simply unfair and simplistic to always blame Israel alone for all problems. Hamas, the terrorist group that controls the Gaza Strip, has launched thousands of rockets into Israeli territory, endangering the lives of innocent civilians. How can the left justify or indirectly support an organization that uses its own population as human shields?

Furthermore, Israel has repeatedly demonstrated its willingness to negotiate and seek a peaceful solution to the conflict. He has made territorial concessions and attempted to establish peace agreements, but has been rejected time and again by Palestinian leaders. Where is the left's criticism of those who refuse to sit at the negotiating table?

It is important to remember that Israel is a democracy, with a free press and an independent judicial system. Israeli citizens have rights and freedoms not found in other countries in the region. However, the left seems to ignore these facts and focus solely on demonizing Israel.

It is understandable that the left wants to defend the oppressed and fight for social justice. But in the case of Israel, this struggle has turned into selective blindness and willful deafness. It is necessary to open your eyes and ears, and examine the situation objectively and balanced.

Indirectly supporting Hamas and blaming Israel alone does not help find a peaceful and lasting solution to the conflict. It is time for the left to recognize the complexity of the situation and seek a more balanced and constructive approach. Only through a strong and secure Jewish State can we advance towards a peace agreement in the Middle East.

In conclusion, the world on the left is blind and deaf when it comes to Israel. It is necessary to break the autopilot that dictates that Israel is guilty of everything. Reality is much more complex and requires an objective and balanced analysis. Indirectly supporting Hamas and demonizing Israel only perpetuates the conflict and makes it difficult to find a peaceful solution. It is time to open our eyes and ears, and work towards lasting peace in the region.

The far left, characterized by its radical ideologies and anti-establishment stance, has often been associated with condemnation of Israel. This condemnation is not surprising, since those who do not believe in freedom and democracy will never support Israel. What is disconcerting, however, is the center-left's flirtation with undemocratic regimes and its lack of support for Israel's right to defend itself. When exploring the reasons behind the automatic condemnation of Israel by the extreme left and the questionable alliance formed with undemocratic regimes, the truth is that it is unusual that there is no analysis or possible questioning.

This alliance with autocratic non-democratic regimes and certainly with Muslim dictatorships is detrimental to the principles of freedom and democracy that the left claims to defend.

Chapter 13: The brutal and baseless condemnation of Israel by the extreme left

The condemnation of Israel by the far left can be attributed to its ideological alignment with anti-imperialism and anti-colonialism. Israel, being a nation born of conflict and colonization, is seen by the far left as an extension of Western imperialism. They argue that the establishment of Israel was the result of the displacement and oppression of the Palestinian people, and therefore must be condemned.

Furthermore, the far left often aligns itself with the Palestinian cause, seeing it as a fight against oppression and occupation. They argue that Israel's policies toward the Palestinians, such as building settlements and restricting movement, are violations of human rights and international law, despite being fully aware that some of these actions serve to prevent civilian deaths. Israelis.

This alignment with the Palestinian cause leads the extreme left to condemn Israel and support the "Palestinian resistance", very often maintaining a complicit silence when this supposed "resistance transforms into clear and pristine terrorism.

An example of the total lack of impartiality and criticism by many as behavior tinged with outright Judeophobia is that of the ultra-left in the European Parliament. The public Spanish newspaper reports: it is about atrocities, false information and a marked anti-Soundism that is nothing other than modern anti-Semitism.

"They have been in Tel Aviv unconditionally supporting a genocidal regime that has turned the Gaza Strip into something very similar to the Warsaw ghetto, subjecting themselves to a siege in which they are being left to die without water, fuel, or medicine, nor food," cried Manu Pineda (IU), who is the head of the European Chamber delegation for relations with Palestine." (52)

And he adds a phrase that according to the modern definition of anti-Semitism cannot be considered anything other than anti-Jewish:"Zionism is a supremacist ideology, the same as the Nazi ideology was."(52)

The United Left leaves no doubt about its markedly anti-Israeli tendency, which according to the IHRA would undoubtedly be classified as anti-Semitic.

While in Argentina the brutal attack by the terrorist group Hamas on the civilian population of Israel motivated national deputies to express themselves in the middle of the special session that was held in Congress, Argentine legislators Romina del Plá and Nicolás del Caño harshly questioned the government of Israel. "There is no doubt that it was this policy (that of the Israeli government) that led the Palestinian population to despair. That is why we, as a political force, unconditionally claim the right to rebellion of the Palestinian people against this decades-long oppression," Del Plá emphasized when speaking during the session. (27)

Added to this is the unusual position of the Chilean communist party, which expressed that it blamed Israel for the horrible massacre of its inhabitants.

"Given the dramatic events that occurred this October 7, which so far have cost the lives of more than 500 victims, we call to remember that the Palestinian people are the object of an occupation."

"The Government headed by Benjamin Netanyahu is responsible for the current situation by encouraging its radical management, including action by armed settlers and occupation forces."(28)

The reflection of the president of the Jewish community of Chile, Ariela Agosin:"Unfortunately in Chile, some politicians, opinion leaders, parliamentarians and communicators – based on a supposed context – have wanted to justify this. I resist living in a society where there is a justification for barbarism, where the law of a tie prevails, the relativization of the value of life, where the massacre of children and the elderly, and the rape of women, is justified. function of what they call "resistance". And it is not enough to say that we are not playing for a tie, when in fact it is." (29)

But precisely in Chile there is also the opposite example, Senator Jaime Quintana, president of the Party for Democracy, has been brave and consistent with the true values of progressivism, being a light in the long night of the left regarding the Middle East.

Senator Quintana stated bravely and consistently in a current tweet: "https://x.com/senadorquintana/status/1710797945912648174?s=20:

"Israel has every right to defend itself from Hamas terrorism and the international community has the duty to promote a lasting understanding that allows peaceful coexistence between both peoples, without further civilian victims."(30)

Even in the United States, the "progressive" Ocasio-Cortez, now considered by many to be markedly anti-Israeli, equates the terrorist group Hamas with the Jewish State, this regrettable action of equating the perpetrator with the victim is completely painful and totally criticizable." Rep. Alexandria Ocasio-Cortez accused Israel of "war crimes" as the close U.S. allay prepares for a possible ground invasion of Gaza amid growing fears of an expanding war."

The New York Democrat and "squad" member condemned "intolerance and insensitivity" at a rally in Times Square just days after the Hamas terrorist attack inside Israel.

But he also called for a ceasefire, and on Sunday characterized both the Hamas attack and Israel's response – which includes cutting off water and power in what the government has called a siege – as war crimes.

When it was still not possible to identify a good part of the children, babies, and young people. Men, women and older adults murdered, beheaded, burned and many dismembered, the Spanish ultra-left called the victims to account and cruelly supported the perpetrator.

The second vice president of the Spanish government and leader of Sumar is one of those at the center of the political storm, and received harsh criticism from the popular and the extreme right, who described her statements as "shameful." He defended that he was "with all the victims" and that it was necessary "to end the occupation so that the Palestinian people can live with dignity."

Sumar's spokesman, Ernest Urtasun, has confirmed this, placing maximum responsibility on the "occupier, Israel" and criticizing the "double standard" of the international community. Podemos spokesperson Isa Serra spoke along the same lines, charging against the Israeli "theocracy" and clarifying that she is "in favor of the Palestinian people" and their right to self-determination. And the CUP demonstrated in Barcelona in favor of Palestine, criticized the "genocide" they suffer and praised the "fight" against "injustice" through the networks, with a "Up with the Palestinian people! To victory!" None has placed emphasis on condemning Hamas.(329)

Radio France International (RFI) reported that "In France the leader of the left did not classify Hamas as a terrorist organization and also disqualified French Jewish leaders."(33)

Expanding RFI, it highlighted that "The president of the Jewish organizations expressed that Mélenchon is "an enemy of the French Republic," the president of the CRIF, Yonatan Arfi, stated on RMC radio, for whom the leftist politician chose to "legitimize terrorism by comparing Israel and Hamas."

RFI found that Prime Minister Élisabeth Borne accused LFI of "hidden" anti-Semitism.

The French media continued describing the controversial and poorly founded statements of the leftist leader and his party "Criticism against the radical left in France points to its rejection, to calling Hamas a "terrorist", and its insistence on remembering the blockade that Israel subdues the Gaza Strip."

To make it clear that Israel and the Jews are always to blame, the LFI party stated: "We will not change even one comma of our position, which is that of the supporters of peace," declared Mathilde Panot, parliamentary leader of LFI.

The Latin American leftists, captured by a principled discourse that does not see what it does not want to see, reacted violently, accusing the victim of being an aggressor, quickly forgetting the torture and killing of children, babies, men, women and the elderly by the "brave Palestinian resistance.

This is how the president of Colombia, Gustavo Petro, accuses Israel of a true genocide and asks his ambassador to return. Bogotá, the president of Chile, calls his ambassador in Israel for Israel's crimes in Gaza and the government of Bolivia once again cuts relations with the Jewish State. (54)(55)(56).

These questionable actions of the Latin American leftist leaders were congratulated and thanked by none other than the terrorist group Hamas itself, an organization that has just perpetrated the largest pogrom in history.

The reflection of Professor Gabriel Zaliasnik in his column "Progressive Betrayal" in the newspaper La Tercera, correctly illustrates the painful question, Was it not enough that the torture and massacre of the Hamas-Isis terrorists was broadcast live on social networks? by the perpetrators themselves?", "harshness towards the victims seems to have not been enough for a part of the left that, without hesitation and with selective blindness, embraces Islamic jihadism and joins its bloody crusade against Israel, the West and civilization Jewish Christian."(54)

Questionable Alliance with undemocratic regimes

While the far left's condemnation of Israel could eventually be understood within the context of its ideological alignment, the alliance formed with undemocratic regimes raises fundamental concerns for progressivism.

The extreme left, which claims to defend freedom and democracy, should be cautious about allying itself with regimes that suppress these same principles while at the same time not watching or listening to what is happening in Muslim countries or addressing the drama of Arab countries in regarding the gender and LGBT agenda at least.

For example, the Cuban dictatorship, led by Fidel Castro and now continued by his brother Raúl, has been a long-standing ally of the far left. Despite its claims to socialist ideals, the Cuban regime has been criticized for its human rights abuses and lack of political freedoms. Similarly, Nicaragua's authoritarian regime, led by Daniel Ortega, has been accused of repressing dissent and undermining democratic institutions.

Venezuela, under the regime of Nicolás Maduro, presents another example of the questionable alliances of the far left. The country has been affected by economic collapse, political repression and human rights violations. The far left's support for the Venezuelan regime, despite its undemocratic practices, raises questions about its commitment to democratic principles.

The left in a cynical way is complicit with its silence in the sad reality in Muslim countries and also in its solidarity with dictatorships.

Chapter 14: The ambiguous behavior of the center-left

What is even more disconcerting is the behavior of the center-left, which often flirts with undemocratic regimes and does not support Israel's right to defend itself. The center-left, which presents itself as a moderate alternative to the extreme left, should defend the principles of freedom, democracy and human rights.

However, in recent years, we have witnessed center-left politicians and parties expressing sympathy towards undemocratic regimes and adopting a critical stance towards Israel. This behavior not only undermines the principles they claim to defend, but also damages their credibility as defenders of democracy.

The newspaper ABC explains very well the contradictions of the leader of the Spanish Socialist Party, Pedro Sanchez: "The President of the Government, Pedro Sánchez, cannot hide that he is in a very uncomfortable position regarding the war between Israel and the Hamas terrorists. Spain was left out of a joint statement issued by the United States, the United Kingdom, France, Italy and Germany a few hours after the brutal attack by Hamas in Israel, two Saturdays ago. Afterwards, it maintained an initial equidistant position, hostage as the PSOE is to its government partners."

The president of the Chilean Community of Israel, Gabriel Colodro, points to the Chilean chancellor, who is theoretically a social democrat in a left-wing government.Alberto van Klaveren recklessly stated: "We call on all parties involved in the acts of violence in Israel and the Palestinian territories to respect that basic principle, that goes for Hamas, Islamic Jihad, the State of Israel and any other actor intervening in the conflict".

Something that, according to Colodro, is practically equaling the State of Israel "With terrorist groups like Hamas and the Palestinian Islamic Jihad, which is absolutely reprehensible and unreal." It is something that we did not see in the reactions of any of the other governments that have They have been very supportive and have well understood the seriousness of the situation, in that sense I believe that the chancellor did not know how to read or convey what he should have done, being a representative of a State friendly to Israel."(35)

Many were surprised by Van Klaveren's unfounded and painful statement, especially when it is known that the Chilean foreign minister comes from a family of Holocaust survivors.

Something similar happened with the President of Brazil, Lula da Silva, who places all actors as responsible without differentiating victims from perpetrators:"or what is happening in the Middle East is a genocide." "It is not a war, it is a genocide that has killed almost 2,000 children who have nothing to do with this war, they are victims of this war. And frankly, I don't know how a human being is capable of waging war knowing that the result of that war is the death of innocent children," he declared.(36)

This response is not uniform or unanimous, for example, after the entire crisis experienced, when the English Labor Party was led by the one accused of being anti-Semitic, Jeremy Corbyn, the current general secretary of that important party, has expressed his full support for the right of Israel. to defend themselves, completely distancing themselves from the anti-Israeli positions that dominated English Labor for a long time." (37)

In conclusion, the condemnation or ambiguity regarding Israel by the moderate left cannot be understood except within a context of ideological and value confusion.

Considering that being on the side of the barbarism and sadism of Hamas or placing the only democracy in the Middle East on a par with a bloodthirsty and murderous group cannot and should not be considered in any case an anti-imperialist and anti-colonialist act.

Everything becomes even more complex when we note the alliance formed with undemocratic regimes. This raises concerns about the left's commitment to freedom and democracy. The center-left flirtatious behavior towards these regimes further undermines their credibility as defenders of democratic principles. It is essential that the left, both the extreme and the center, reevaluate their alliances and prioritize the principles of freedom, democracy and human rights.

Only then can they understand that what is truly progressive is to genuinely and truly support Israel's right to defend itself from the monstrous threat of Iran and its murderous proxies like Hamas or Hezbollah.

The hypocritical attitude of the left towards Islam: women and homosexuals

As we have reiterated in previous paragraphs, we have witnessed in recent years a growing concern for the rights of women and the LGBTQ+ community. However, it is surprising to see how the political left, which calls itself defenders of these groups, shows a hypocritical attitude when it comes to addressing problems related to Islam.

This brutal contradiction of the left, which has adopted an incoherent position on issues such as the rights of women and the LGBTQ+ community when confronting Islam.

The left's hypocrisy becomes evident when examining its attitude towards women's rights in the context of Islam. While the left presents itself as a defender of gender equality and women's reproductive rights, it appears to ignore or minimize the discriminatory and oppressive practices that occur in some Islamic communities. For example, veiling, female genital mutilation, and forced marriages are practices that violate women's fundamental rights, but are often overlooked or justified by the left in the name of cultural tolerance.

Furthermore, the left has shown an ambiguous attitude towards the LGBTQ+ community when it comes to Islam. While the left has been a champion of the rights of this community, it has been notably silent regarding the persecution and discrimination that LGBTQ+ people suffer in Islamic countries.

In many Muslim countries, homosexuality is illegal and punishable by penalties ranging from prison to the death penalty. However, the left seems to avoid criticizing these practices for fear of being accused of Islamophobia.

This hypocritical attitude of the left is based on a misinterpretation of cultural tolerance. While it is important to respect and value cultural differences, this should not mean ignoring or justifying practices that violate fundamental human rights.

The left has fallen into the trap of relativizing the rights of women and the LGBTQ+ community in the name of cultural diversity, which undermines its own fight for equality and social justice.

The hypocritical attitude of the left towards Islam on issues related to the rights of women and the LGBTQ+ community is a contradiction that cannot be ignored. If the left aims to be a champion of equality and social justice, it must be consistent in its fight for the rights of all groups, including women and LGBTQ+ people.

Cultural tolerance should not be used as an excuse to justify oppressive and discriminatory practices. It is time for the left to reflect on its position and commit to defending universal human rights, regardless of the culture or religion of the people involved.

The question asked by Professor Gabriel Zaliasnik is devastating and devastating for those who adhere to or sympathize with the left: "At what time and why did that supposedly secular and progressive world adopt the imposture of misogynistic and totalitarian ideologies?" (54)

Chapter 15: Academia and the double standard when it comes to Israel: an intellectual shame that falls into the anti-Jewish trap of BDS

In academia, researchers and academics are expected to be impartial and objective in their studies and analysis. However, when it comes to Israel, there is often a double standard that undermines intellectual integrity and falls into the trap of anti-Jewish propaganda. This double standard is an intellectual embarrassment and must be addressed urgently and with critical thinking.

The double standard in academia is manifested in the way the Israel-Palestine conflict is addressed. While other conflicts in the world receive balanced attention and are analyzed from different perspectives, the Israeli-Palestinian conflict is often presented in a biased and one-sided manner. Academics who are supposed to be impartial often take an anti-Israel stance without considering the facts and complexities of the conflict.

This double standard is evident in the way Israel is criticized disproportionately compared to other countries. For example, Israel is criticized for its response to terrorist attacks, while other countries facing similar threats are rarely questioned. This lack of fairness in analysis undermines the credibility of the academic community and shows a clear anti-Jewish bias.

Furthermore, the double standard manifests itself in the demonization of Israel and the denial of its right to exist as a Jewish state. A level of moral perfection is required of Israel that is not expected of other countries. Not only is this unfair, it is also a reflection of deep-seated prejudices and a lack of objectivity in academia.

BDS, the origin of anti-Semitic hatred and Judeophobia

As Natan Sharansky explains, "the Boycott, Divestment and Sanctions (BDS) movement has gained popularity in recent years, attracting many who believe they are fighting for human rights and seeking a solution to the conflict between Israel and Palestine. However, the truth is that BDS has only one goal: the destruction of the State of Israel. This objective is cleverly hidden under the guise of the fight for human rights and legitimate criticism of Israel."(66)

- Sharansky states that "for thousands of years, the demonization of the Jewish people has been a widely used tactic. Jews have been accused of blood libels, poisoning wells and controlling the global banking system. These unfounded accusations have led to persecution and violence against Jews throughout history."(68)

"The delegitimization of Jewish faith and nationality has also been a strategy used to discriminate and marginalize Jews. At certain periods in history, they were denied recognition of their nationality and stripped of their rights and property. This delegitimization has led to the exclusion and oppression of Jews in different societies."(67)

The application of double standards towards Jews is another form of anti-Semitism. Throughout history, special laws and discriminatory policies have been imposed against them, either in the form of segregationist or de facto laws. This double standard has resulted in discrimination and persecution towards Jews in different contexts.

- The demonization of the Jewish people, the delegitimization of their faith and nationality, and the application of double standards have created conditions conducive to pogroms, expulsions and genocides throughout history. These tactics have been used to justify violence and oppression against Jews, and BDS is nothing more than a continuation of this strategy.

- BDS presents itself as a fight for human rights and a legitimate criticism of Israel, but in reality it is a tool to demonize, delegitimize and apply double standards towards the State of Israel and the Jewish people. Behind its apparent justice and solidarity, BDS seeks the destruction of Israel and does not contribute to a peaceful and just solution to the conflict between Israel and Palestine.

It is important to recognize the true intentions behind BDS and not be fooled by its rhetoric. Peace and justice will only be achieved through dialogue and negotiation, not through the demonization and delegitimization of a State and its people.

The anti-Jewish trap that academia falls into is evident in the way terminology is used and facts are distorted to present Israel as solely to blame for the conflict. Terms such as "apartheid" and "genocide" are used to describe the situation in Israel, completely ignoring the complexity of the situation and the existence of a long-standing conflict.

This biased and anti-Jewish approach in academia is not only an intellectual disgrace, but also has negative consequences on society at large. By perpetuating stereotypes and prejudices, hatred and discrimination towards the Jewish community is fueled. Furthermore, the possibility of a constructive dialogue and a peaceful solution to the conflict is undermined.

The double standard in academia when it comes to Israel is an intellectual embarrassment that falls into the anti-Jewish trap. It is essential that academics and researchers strive to be impartial and objective in their analysis, especially when dealing with complex conflicts such as the Israeli-Palestinian conflict.

Only through a balanced and fact-based approach and not the prejudice of the new anti-Semitism called anti-sonism can a deeper understanding and a peaceful solution be achieved. It is the responsibility of the academic community to address this double standard practiced against Israel and work toward greater intellectual integrity.

But in addition, the countries that boycott Israel will be significantly harmed, former Chilean deputy Gabriel Silber explains that it could have a very negative effect. A lot, mainly in technological issues related to the development of our country's infrastructure, for example those related to the use of a resource as important as water."(69)

Chapter 16: Hamas pro-terrorism groups in American universities have been tolerated: the perverse strategy of BDS

In recent years, there has been growing concern about tolerance toward Hamas pro-terrorism groups at universities. This situation has led many professors to make the difficult decision to resign from their academic positions, even at prestigious institutions such as Harvard or UCLA. Certainly, tolerance towards these groups in universities is unacceptable and must be urgently addressed.

The financial newspaper reports that "the prestigious Harvard University[1] has been embroiled in controversy, after more than 30 student groups issued a controversial statement blaming Israel for the escalation of violence in the war against Hamas[2]".

It all started when a coalition of Harvard student groups published a collective message titled: "Joint Statement of the Harvard Palestine Solidarity Groups on the Situation in Palestine" on The Harvard Crimson site, in which some members of the student community accused Israel of being "entirely responsible" for the attacks that have left thousands of victims since last weekend."

The Palestinian Hamas terrorists had not yet finished their orgy of torture and pain, they continued burning bodies and mutilating corpses when these truly heartless organizations blamed Israel for the horrific carnage that had occurred."(38)

Also using terms that have been applied to Jews for centuries, such as ghetto. This makes it even more painful. Yes, Harvard alumni reacted to these unusual statements

Former Treasury Secretary Lawrence Summers, who was president of that university, said he was "outraged" not only by the statement, but by "the silence of Harvard leaders." Harvard seems "at best, neutral in the face of acts of terrorism against the Jewish State of Israel," it noted on its X network account (formerly Twitter).(39)

For his part, the Democratic congressman from Massachusetts, Jake Auchincloss, maintained that he was "ashamed" of his university, describing the associations' text as "morally depraved" and the position of the leaders as "moral cowardice."(39)

These student-led groups across the United States supported Palestine amid Israel's invasion over the weekend, and some appeared to applaud the attack by the terrorist organization Hamas. That is to say, while entire families were cruelly massacred, there were those who considered that the victims were to blame for the horrific mass rapes and sadistic torture of the Hamas-Isis terrorist group.

Student organizations in the United States signed a letter holding the Israeli regime responsible for all the violence that is unfolding.

"Today's events did not occur in a vacuum," the letter reads. Yale University students clashed with their Ivy League counterparts over the weekend. Yalies4Palestine wrote in a statement that Palestinians "made history this Saturday morning when they tore down the wall that has imprisoned Gaza for 17 years."

"The events of October 7 are not an isolated event, but the inevitable result of a decades-long apartheid and suffocating blockade, coupled with a year of escalating settler violence against civilians in the West Bank," Yalies4Palestine said. "The resistance is the consequence of long-standing and ongoing Zionist colonization."

Considering "resistance" when cutting the throats of babies, raping women and girls, and kidnapping Holocaust survivors, demonstrates a total lack of sensitivity and a brutal inability to have a reasonable and relatively impartial position in the conflicts of the Middle East.

1. https://www.elfinanciero.com.mx/mundo/2023/07/04/escandalo-en-harvard-acusan-a-la-universidad-de-racismo-y-de-nepotismo/

2. https://www.elfinanciero.com.mx/mundo/2023/10/12/hamas-pide-a-israel-detener-ataques-a-civiles-en-gaza-es-pronto-para-hablar-de-liberar-rehenes/

The Catholic News Agency reported that "While Israel was still searching and unfortunately finding the bodies of entire families riddled in their beds," some of the student leaders allowed themselves to repeat lies, attack the victims for their alleged complicity and even support the group. Hamas terrorist.

There is no doubt that the sad spectacle of several North American universities will not be easily forgotten.

Not all authorities reacted passively, on the contrary, some took radical decisions, such as the Governor of Florida:

"Florida Republican Gov. Ron DeSantis' administration has taken the unprecedented step of forcing the state's universities to ban a pro-Palestinian student club, alleging that the group illegally supports Hamas terrorists who attacked Israel earlier this year. this month".

Some students have shown support for the Palestinians as Israel's attacks on Hamas intensified, drawing harsh criticism from some Jewish academics and even some potential employers. The state of Florida, however, has gone even further, labeling Students for Justice in Palestine as an organization it considers a terrorist group.

At DeSantis' request, Chancellor Ray Rodrigues of the State University System wrote to university presidents ordering them to disband SJP chapters. He refers to the national organization's statement that "Palestinian students in exile are part of this movement, not in solidarity with this movement."

"Knowingly providing material support to a designated foreign terrorist organization" is a crime in Florida, Rodrigues states in the letter.(40)

Other authorities tried to distance themselves from what was happening on their Campuses. For example, according to *Financial Times*, the president of the University of Pennsylvania, Liz Magill, said that her institution "strongly opposes Hamas terrorist attacks in Israel and anti-Semitism" and likewise recognized that "We should have communicated our position more quickly and more widely."(41)

BDS: the new anti-Semitism that paves the way to hatred and Judeophobia

"Those who argue that the massacre perpetrated by Hamas and the painful support that this group that is equal to Isis has had did not occur in a vacuum are right, of course for absolutely different reasons than those they argue."

· Indeed, the disastrous work of the Boycott, Divestment and Sanctions against Israel has paid off. BDS has managed to revive hatred of Israel and Jews in an incredibly efficient way.

· Natán Sharansky explains: "The Boycott, Divestment and Sanctions movement uses historical tools of anti-Semitism to seek the elimination of the Jewish State."(68)

First, it is important to note that tolerance toward Hamas pro-terrorism groups on campuses is rooted in the hate work of BDS.

What these modern anti-Semites have accomplished goes against the fundamental principles of higher education. Academic institutions have a responsibility to encourage critical thinking, open debate and diversity of opinions. However, allowing the presence of groups that support terrorism undermines these principles by promoting violence and intolerance rather than constructive dialogue.

· Additionally, tolerance toward these groups can have negative consequences for the safety and well-being of the university community. Support for terrorism not only endangers the lives of students and teachers, but also creates an environment of fear and hostility that makes learning and the exchange of ideas difficult.

It is the responsibility of universities to ensure a safe and conducive environment for the academic and personal development of their members, and allowing the presence of Hamas pro-terrorism groups goes against this objective.

Likewise, tolerating these groups can have a negative impact on the reputation of universities. Institutions such as Harvard or UCLA are recognized worldwide for their academic excellence and their commitment to democratic values. However, allowing the presence of pro-terrorism groups risks damaging the image of these institutions and undermining their credibility. This can have long-term consequences, such as a decline in the quality of students and teachers who choose these universities, as well as the loss of public funding and support.

Finally, it is important to highlight that tolerance towards Hamas pro-terrorism groups in universities is not a legitimate exercise of freedom of expression. While it is true that freedom of expression is a fundamental right, it also has limits.

Supporting terrorism and promoting violence cannot be considered a valid form of expression, since it violates human rights and people's safety. It is the responsibility of universities to set clear boundaries and ensure that freedom of expression is exercised respectfully.

In conclusion, tolerance towards Hamas pro-terrorism groups in universities is unacceptable and must be urgently addressed. This situation goes against the fundamental principles of higher education, endangers the safety and well-being of the university community, damages the reputation of academic institutions and cannot be considered a legitimate form of freedom of expression.

It is the responsibility of universities to take firm measures to ensure a safe, inclusive and respectful academic environment, in which constructive dialogue is promoted and any form of support for terrorism and anti-Semitism and Judeophobia is rejected.

Chapter 17: The appalling and absolutely unacceptable UN double standard

Systematic discrimination against Israel at the United Nations is a matter of great controversy and concern. The United Nations (UN) has adopted a double standard in its treatment of Israel, which has led to a series of unfair resolutions and actions against it. In this essay, we will look at some examples of how the UN discriminates against Israel and how this affects equity and justice in the international system.

One of the main problems is the UN General Assembly, which adopts around 20 resolutions against Israel each year, while only adopting 5 to 6 resolutions against the rest of the world combined. This clearly shows a bias and double standard against Israel. Furthermore, the General Assembly does not adopt any resolutions on countries that are systematic violators of human rights, such as Cuba, China or Saudi Arabia. This demonstrates a lack of fairness and justice in the UN's treatment of Israel.

Other UN bodies, such as the Commission on the Status of Women (CSW) and the World Health Organization (WHO), also show a bias against Israel. These organizations condemn only Israel at their annual meetings, ignoring human rights violations in other countries. For example, the CSW condemns Israel, but ignores violations of women's rights in Saudi Arabia, where the male guardian system is extremely restrictive and women face discrimination and lack of rights.

Similarly, the WHO condemns Israel, but ignores the massive health crises in countries like Syria and Venezuela. This clearly shows a double standard and lack of fairness in the UN's treatment of Israel.

The UN Human Rights Council (HRC) also shows bias and double standards against Israel. In each session of the HRC, Israel is the only country that is discussed under a special item for a specific country, while the rest of the countries and their human rights situations are discussed under a general item that applies to all countries. Furthermore, Israel is condemned in at least 5 resolutions each year, while countries like Syria, Iran and North Korea, which are systematic violators of human rights, are only the subject of 1 or 2 resolutions. This clearly shows a bias and double standard in the UN's treatment of Israel.

For UN Watch, furthermore, the tone of the resolutions against Israel is different from that of resolutions against other countries. The anti-Israel resolutions are full of biased hyperbole and systematically suppress facts that could contradict the anti-Israel narrative. On the other hand, resolutions against other countries contain praise and support for the governments. This clearly shows a bias in the language and tone of UN resolutions.

Rovner explains that another example of discrimination against Israel is the UN Special Rapporteur on Palestine. This expert has a biased mandate that allows him to condemn only Israel for human rights violations, while completely ignoring violations committed by the other party to the conflict. This clearly shows a bias and double standard in the UN's treatment of Israel "And could be seen as having by omission covered up Hamas with the horrible results for the whole world to see."

This bias becomes even more important after the tendentious and dangerous speech of the UN Secretary General, Guterres, who in a certain way justifies the barbaric massacre of Hamas, by stating "Hamas' actions did not occur in a vacuum." (60) And he is absolutely right, except that he points, like almost his entire organization, to the victim and cowardly sympathizes with the perpetrator, but he is right, the Palestinian leaders paved the way for this massacre to occur.

The curricula of Hamas and the Palestinian Authority continue to be based on hatred of Jews, the glorification of terrorists, calling them martyrs and the well-known PA policy of paying a lifetime pension to those who kill Jews, the financing of terrorism by Western governments and the questioned work of UNRWA (59) are effectively where we can try to understand what happened that Black Saturday.

It is possible that Guterres is the same as many world leaders, he does not know or understand what anti-Semitism is and he is probably not fully aware that his actions could qualify as anti-Jewish, Judeophobic or anti-Semitic.

This is why Israel and Jewish organizations in general have cut ties with Guterres. For example, the International Raoul Wallenberg Foundation has revoked the Honorary Membership of the UN Secretary General, Antonio Guterres. (42)

The decision was made by the IRWF Board of Directors following Mr. Guterres' recent statement, in which he stated that "the Hamas attack did not occur in a vacuum."

Mr. Baruj Tenembaum, founder of the foundation, sent a letter to Mr. Guterres, stating that "his statement goes beyond what is acceptable and strongly contradicts the spirit of the International Raoul Wallenberg Foundation and the values defended by the Swedish hero." .

In short, the UN systematically discriminates against Israel through a marked and constant double standard.

UN Watch Legal Advisor Dina Rovner for panel on double standards against Israel (44)

The unfortunate performance of the UN is unfortunately not a temporary problem. On the contrary, it has been constantly repeated for years.

Rovner emphasizes "I'm going to start with item 7 on the agenda." In each session of the Human Rights Council there are 10 items on the agenda. Israel is the only country that is discussed under a special item for a specific country – item 7. All other countries and their human rights situations are discussed under item 4, which applies to all countries."

Resolutions: Every year at the Human Rights Council, Israel is condemned in at least 5 resolutions, while there are only 3 on Syria, where hundreds of thousands have been killed and millions have been displaced. Other countries such as Iran, which executes children, North Korea, which holds tens of thousands as political prisoners in prison camps, and Myanmar, which is accused of genocide against the Muslim Rohingya, are the subject of 1 or 2 resolutions per year, and some of the worst abusers such as China, Cuba, Russia and Saudi Arabia are not singled out in any resolution."(63)

Rovner delves into "Tone of the resolutions"."The resolutions on Israel are covered in biased hyperbole and systematically suppress facts that could contradict or show a context that could offer balance, while the resolutions on the other countries contain praise and support for the governments."

Then, the legal advisor of UN Watch emphasizes "Then we have the sessions, Israel has been the subject of more special sessions at the Human Rights Council than any other country. In the first six months of the Council, during the height of the crisis in Darfur, the Council organized 3 special sessions on Israel and only 1 on Darfur. By the end of 2009, half of the HRC special sessions had been on Israel." The UN watch lawyer explains.

Then, Dina Rovner explains about the functioning of the Investigation Commissions: "Similarly, there have been more commissions of inquiry into Israel than into any other country. And all of these investigative commissions receive biased mandates that prejudge Israel's guilt and give a free pass to Hamas and other terrorist groups."

This is extremely serious, warns Rovner. "For example, resolution S-28/1, which created the commission of inquiry into the Return Marches in Gaza, called for an investigation into the context of "Israel's military assault against large-scale civilian protests." scale," and did not mention Hamas. "He also assumed that war crimes had been committed." Rovner places special emphasis on the Special Rapporteur on Palestine, explaining what "The UN has 9 experts on specific country situations. But only the expert on Palestine has a biased mandate that allows him to condemn only one side of the conflict for violations – Israel – and completely ignore violations committed by the other side of the conflict."

Going deeper, Rovner details about the language of the mandate, "to investigate Israel's violations of the principles and foundations of international law..." So every time we ask Michael Lynk – who is the current Special Rapporteur on Palestine – Why does he not address Palestinian violations of human rights such as arbitrary arrests, torture, censorship by the Palestinian Authority and Hamas? His response is always the same: that is outside my mandate.

CEDR assessment on Palestine

"That was just a quick look at some of the double standards that exist at the UN. Of course, there are many other examples," says UN Watch.

It explains the sad reality of this gigantic organization. "What I just summarized shows how the UN system is completely tilted against Israel" Rovner states.

This NGO has set itself a goal: that "the UN investigates and condemns Palestinian violations of human rights."

Palestine became a non-member state of the UN in 2012. Then, in April 2014, the Palestinian Authority signed five human rights treaties, including the Convention on the Elimination of Racial Discrimination – the convention against racism.

These treaties have committees of experts that evaluate each State's compliance every certain regular period of time. Therefore, by signing these treaties, the Palestinian Authority is subjecting itself to the evaluation process that is supposed to hold governments accountable for failing to comply with the treaties." Aim UN Watch.

And as befits any country, the Palestinians are beginning to be evaluated by these commissions – which means that these bodies should hold them accountable for their violations. "The anti-racism committee's evaluation took place in August. The evaluation was to address Palestinian compliance with the anti-racism convention." "You don't have to look far to find all kinds of anti-Semitic incitement from Palestinians, just read the public statements of Palestinian officials, look at the media of the Palestinian Authority and Hamas, and the Palestinian educational curriculum." (44)

The widespread anti-Semitism of Palestinian society, "we were surprised to find that the report presented by the Palestinian Authority before the committee repeatedly blamed the "Israeli occupation" for countless violations of Palestinian rights, while seeking to evade any responsibility for its own racism. and discrimination," explains the UN Watch expert.

There was a complete denial of racism among Palestinians. The AP report even said that it "had not detected racist discourse in Palestinian society."

- Instead of acknowledging its own anti-Semitic and terrorist incitement, the PA report accuses Israel of inciting racial discrimination and violence against Palestinians.

- The Palestinian Authority report ignored attacks by Palestinians against Jews praying at Jewish holy sites, while accusing Israel of preventing Palestinians from exercising their religious rights. Nor did he talk about his own violence and discrimination against Christians.

- The PA report does not address the fact that no Jews live in Palestinian-controlled territory, even though 21% of Israel's population is Arab.

Ultimately, the Palestinians were doing more of the same at the UN, taking advantage of the anti-racism committee's reporting processes as another UN vehicle to attack Israel while it shied away from its obligations. But in this case, they were appearing before a group of experts that has the explicit mandate to observe the performance of the Palestinians on the issue of racism.

The deficiencies of the Palestinian Authority report were pointed out and its hypocrisy and double-standards were exposed. Advisor UN Watch Legal Dina Rovner states: "In a private meeting with committee members, where we were accompanied by NGO Monitor and the organization Impact-SE as well as a representative of the pro-Palestinian NGO Al-Haq, we were able to have an intimate face-to-face conversation. Face with some of the committee members.

We were able to remind them again and again that the evaluation was about Palestine, not Israel. We were able to answer their questions and respond to some absurd statements expressed by Al-Haq representatives.

And when the official evaluation began later, we could already see our impact when members of the committee asked the Palestinian Authority tough questions like the following:

- How do you explain the anti-Semitic incitement in the Palestinian media in the statements of public officials?

- What is the AP planning to deal with anti-Semitism in textbooks?

- Is there a Jewish minority in Palestine?

- How are Jews and other minorities represented in the media?

The representative of the PA spoke, he could not answer the questions why it is a fact that if someone applies ethnic cleansing it is the Palestinian Authority

It should be noted that this time at least the committee did not accept the Palestinians' invitation to turn the evaluation into another attack against Israel. And in his concluding remarks, which were published a few weeks later, he urged Palestinians to combat hate speech and incitement to violence, noting the conclusion that hate speech against Israelis "promotes hatred and can incite to violence and anti-Semitism." The report specifies, in a very unusual summary of the United Nations.

UN Committee condemns Israel 8 times, and the rest of the world 0 times[3]

The result is so absurd, also knowing what is happening in Syria, Iran, Lebanon, Palestine or in Latin America in Cuba, Venezuela or Nicaragua, and of course in North Korea or Afghanistan. The double standard and institutional discrimination against Israel is brutal.(63)

But unfortunately this is not a particular event, there is a long history of negative discrimination by the UN towards the Jewish state.

The relationship between Israel and Arab countries within the United Nations has been the subject of controversy, especially regarding the disproportionate resolutions adopted against Israel.

Until 1990, of a total of 175 Security Council resolutions, 97 were voted against Israel, revealing a significant disparity. This disproportionate number has raised concerns about the objectivity and impartiality of the resolutions directed at Israel.

Similarly, in the General Assembly, of the 690 resolutions adopted through 1990, 429 were voted against Israel. This overwhelming majority suggests an anti-Israel bias within the United Nations.

---

3.   https://unwatch.org/comite-de-la-onu-condena-8-veces-a-israel-y-0-al-resto-del-mundo/

An additional problem was the silence of the United Nations when it came to violations of Jewish heritage committed by Arab countries. For example, when Jordan destroyed 58 synagogues in Jerusalem, the UN remained silent and did not issue condemnations or take meaningful action.

Nor did the UN speak out when the ancient Jewish cemetery on the Mount of Olives was desecrated by the Jordanians, which also went unnoticed by the United Nations, increasing the perception of selective inaction.

Furthermore, apartheid-like policies imposed by Jordan, which restricted Jewish access to the Temple Mount and the Western Wall, were ignored by the United Nations. This lack of recognition raises questions about the organization's commitment to defending religious freedom and equality.

These examples highlight a clear bias against Israel and the Jewish people within the United Nations. Critics argue that such bias undermines the organization's credibility and its ability to achieve fair and objective resolutions.

It is important to keep in mind that the resolutions and actions of the United Nations are influenced by the participation and interests of the member states, which, as has been clearly demonstrated, the world organization has acted with a clear anti-Israeli bias.

Shameful appointment: Iran will chair the UN Social Forum on Human Rights

Infobae reports on the unusual decision to appoint the representative of the tyrannical regime of Iran, Ali Bahreini despite the violations of the Persian regime.(66)

According to Infobae, "Iran will assume the presidency of a UN human rights forum on Thursday, sparking an international protest campaign by human rights activists who claim that Tehran's history of oppression, torture and executions makes it unsuitable." "Is suitable for the position."

UNESCO

All United Nations organizations have the same discourse and attitude against the Jewish State, but the truth, the absurdity of what UNESCO resolved, seems insurmountable.

"UNESCO, an organization with extensive anti-Israeli, read Judeophobic, resolutions, issued a document on October 13 stating that the Temple Mount and the Kotel, or Western Wall, also called the Wailing Wall next to the tomb of the Patriarchs, in the city of Hebron, and the tomb of the matriarch Rachel, in Bethlehem, must be removed from the list of sacred places of the Jewish people".

Of course, he does not miss the opportunity to criticize and if possible denigrate the Jewish State. Among other things, it also defines the State of Israel every time it is mentioned as an occupying power, and calls sacred sites by their Arabic name only.

In short, it questions the history and identity of the Jewish people. UNESCO questions Israel's relationship with the Western Wall. Furthermore, it orders Israel to cease archaeological works and constructions; among others, those that involve improvements for, for example, the plaza in front of the Western Wall, the most sacred place for Judaism, which should also be removed from the list of sacred places for Judaism.

Sadly, UNESCO, an organization run by misogynistic and dictatorial regimes such as Iran, Saudi Arabia, Qatar, Pakistan, Sudan and several others, has specialized in condemning Israel with increasing frequency, although the most dangerous thing is that many of these countries They are active financiers of international terrorism.

Chapter 18: Morocco, Egypt, Bahrain, Arab Emirates, Sudan and Jordan: Between peace with Israel and the fear of Islamic fundamentalism that can destabilize them - A complex game

Peace between Israel and some Arab countries has been a major issue in the Middle East for decades. Morocco, Egypt and Jordan are three nations that have established peace agreements with Israel, but at the same time face the fear of being destabilized by Islamic fundamentalism. This argumentative essay will analyze the complexity of this situation, highlighting the challenges these countries face in balancing peace with Israel and the fight against Islamic extremism.

Morocco, Egypt and Jordan have been pioneers in seeking peace with Israel in the Middle East. These agreements have allowed the establishment of diplomatic relations, commercial exchange and cooperation in various areas. However, these countries also face the challenge of maintaining internal stability and preventing Islamic fundamentalism from infiltrating their societies.

The fear of Islamic fundamentalism is understandable, as this movement has proven to be a threat to peace and stability in the region. Extremist groups such as Al-Qaeda and the Islamic State have carried out terrorist attacks in several Arab countries, sowing chaos and violence. It is therefore crucial that Morocco, Egypt and Jordan take measures to prevent radicalization and counter the influence of these groups.

Despite the challenges, these countries have implemented effective strategies to confront Islamic fundamentalism.

They have strengthened their security forces, improved intelligence and promoted education and interfaith dialogue. In addition, they have sought the support of the international community to combat extremism and have participated in regional coalitions to jointly address this problem.

However, peace with Israel has also generated internal tensions in these countries. Some sectors of society oppose the peace agreements, arguing that no significant progress has been made in resolving the Israeli-Palestinian conflict. These critical voices fear that the normalization of relations with Israel will weaken the Palestinian cause and undermine the Arab and Islamic identity of these countries.

It is important to highlight that peace with Israel does not mean that these countries have abandoned their support for the Palestinian cause or that they definitely do not maintain anti-Semitism in their curricula. They have maintained their commitment to the creation of an independent Palestinian state and have advocated for a negotiated solution to the conflict. At the same time, they have recognized that peace with Israel can bring economic and political benefits, and they have sought to take advantage of these opportunities for the development of their nations.

In short, Morocco, Egypt and Jordan find themselves in a complex situation, balancing peace with Israel and fear of Islamic fundamentalism.

These countries have demonstrated their commitment to stability and the fight against extremism, implementing effective strategies to prevent radicalization. At the same time, they have sought to maintain their support for the Palestinian cause and reap the benefits of peace with Israel. Although challenges remain, these countries continue to work to ensure peace and security in the Middle East region.

Chapter 19: Saudi Arabia: Dilemma in which it must choose what is best for its people or those blinded by its anti-Semitism

Saudi Arabia finds itself at a crossroads, facing an ethical and moral dilemma in which it must decide between what is best for its people and those who are blinded by their anti-Semitism.

Saudi Arabia is known for being a country with a strong Islamic influence and a conservative society. However, in recent years there has been a rise in global awareness about the importance of tolerance and respect towards all religions and cultures. In this context, anti-Semitism has become an issue of concern, as it promotes discrimination and hatred towards Jews.

On the one hand, Saudi Arabia must consider what is best for its people. This involves guaranteeing the security and well-being of its citizens, as well as promoting peace and stability in the region. In this sense, it is important that the country moves away from anti-Semitism and promotes religious tolerance. This would allow greater integration into the international community and an improvement in diplomatic relations with other countries.

On the other hand, Saudi Arabia must also deal with those blinded by its anti-Semitism. These people may have deep-rooted beliefs and deep prejudices, making it difficult for them to accept religious diversity. However, it is the responsibility of the Saudi government to educate its population and promote a more open and respectful mindset. This can be achieved through educational programs that foster tolerance and interfaith understanding.

Importantly, anti-Semitism not only affects Jews, but also has a negative impact on society as a whole. It encourages discrimination and exclusion, which can lead to social tensions and conflicts. It is therefore essential that Saudi Arabia takes measures to combat anti-Semitism and promote equal rights and opportunities for all its citizens.

In conclusion, Saudi Arabia faces a dilemma in which it must choose what is best for its people or those blinded by its anti-Semitism. While deep-seated beliefs and prejudices understandably exist, it is the responsibility of the Saudi government to promote religious tolerance and combat anti-Semitism. This will allow for greater integration into the international community and an improvement in diplomatic relations. By doing so, Saudi Arabia will be working towards a more inclusive and respectful future for all its citizens.

Chapter 20: Israel does NOT have a partner today to build a future of peace

The problem faced by those who want a negotiation between Israel and Palestine to move towards a peace process is that a Palestinian group or organization really wants to recognize the right to exist of the Jewish people. We have already been notified that neither Hamas, nor Islamic Jihad, neither the Palestinian Liberation Front, nor the PLO and nor the Palestinian Authority. So with whom? That should be the great concern not only of the countries that have made peace with Israel or rather have normalized their diplomatic relations with the Jewish State, but it should not be the obsession of the progressive world, of the true transformative left and also of the great powers. .

How can we have the Palestinian Authority as a partner that pays a subsidy to those who murder Israelis and if they die the lifetime pension is paid to their family?

But in addition, the president of the Palestinian Authority is, as Hernan López and Gabriel Colodro explain, a Holocaust denier "When Mahmud Abbas blames European Jewry for having generated the Shoah, the Holocaust, with its actions, he crosses the line of morality. Because? Because he lies!"(70)

Both the countries with which Israel has normalized its relations, such as Egypt, Jordan, Morocco or the Arab Emirates and Bahrain, are waiting for their relations with the Jewish State, they need to find a partner for peace.

Not only have many Israeli children been left orphaned after the brutal attack by Hamas, progressivism and the Israeli left have also been left without families. On the one hand, there is no trustworthy partner on the Palestinian side. And on the other hand, the attitude and resolution of the left and progressivism in general to blame Israel directly or indirectly for the massacre perpetrated mainly with those who worked with Palestinians, whether to support them and obtain medical treatment or were working on a peace project. That dream was also cruelly murdered by the barbarism and sadism of terrorism and it will be impossible for it to be resurrected with the same actors.

Israel left Gaza in 2015, the cowardly and murderous attack that was perpetrated in an Israeli territory that Israel has dominated since 1948, has nothing to do with the green line or the 1967 borders. That is, neither the leftist and progressive rhetoric that discusses the sovereignty of certain territories conquered in the six-day war could somehow see this attack from a different perspective. But the ferocity, sadism and deliberate action of torturing the Jews makes it impossible for anyone in Israel to put into perspective what was a real carnage.

Probably and unfortunately, the murderous terrorism of Hamas has had a short-term success in postponing peace between Israel and Saudi Arabia, possibly it has also buried for a long time the possible peace between Israelis and Palestinians. The wound is very deep and will probably leave scars that will not heal in the long term.

Ironically, Israel has received a brutal blow that has caused pain and deep sorrow, but possibly the biggest losers in the long term are the Palestinians themselves, who will see their cause definitively tinged with terrorism and probably because Israel's attitude towards to deliver electricity, water, gas and humanitarian aid, will change. Definitely, in addition, medical treatments for Palestinians in Israeli hospitals will be increasingly limited and it is certainly not clear whether Israel will allow the entry of Palestinian workers or will definitely choose to let in Chinese, Filipinos and other countries that want to come to occupy those positions.

· Israel feels that it has no responsibility towards those who want to exterminate the people and neither towards those who vote for them.

· Definitely, Israel and the Jewish people suffered a blow, a brutal attack that ended the lives of young people, children and adults and the Palestinians lost all credibility to be partners for peace.

Chapter 21: Proportionality, the true concept that exists in the conventions that regulate wars

Without a doubt, the conflict between Israel and Hamas raises a series of complex legal aspects, which must be analyzed in depth. Below, we will explore the key legal issues related to this dispute and the applicable legal principles.

First, it is essential to highlight that Hamas' deliberate violent attacks against Israeli citizens, both civilians and soldiers, constitute serious violations of international law and international criminal law. These acts, such as murders, kidnappings, torture and looting, are considered war crimes and crimes against humanity. Therefore, Hamas has the unavoidable obligation to immediately release all those kidnapped in the Gaza Strip, since their detention is a war crime.(75)

- Nobody asks the attacked Ukraine to react proportionally to the attacks and aggression of Russia, it would hardly have been possible for the United States to react proportionally to the cowardly attack on Pearl Harbor and very few actually asked it in the face of the horrific terrorist attacks of September 11, 2001 perpetrated by Al Queda under the sinister direction of Osama Bin Laden.

- One could mistakenly believe, by the way, what proportionality it is that if Hamas terrorists went house to house in 22 villages and kibbutzim raping, murdering, torturing and burning babies, Israel should do the same.

- Would proportionality be, according to that logic, firing 15,000 missiles trying to kill civilians, would it be proportional?

- Jose I. Rodríguez, in the electronic newspaper Aurora, reflects on what a "proportional reaction" is required of Israel. Rodríguez affirms "a proportional response from Israel to the massacre that Hamas has produced in the last hours, would have to vilely and cowardly murder entire families, father, mother, sons and daughters, grandchildren and even grandparents in their own beds within their houses."(47)

- "If Israel has to respond proportionally to the massacre that Hamas has produced, it would have to brutally torture, rape and drag the women it has kidnapped." Israel has the most ethical and moral army in the world. The Israel Defense Forces would never do what Hamas did to men, women, children and the elderly.(47)

- And he adds "If Israel has to respond proportionally to the massacre that Hamas has caused by invading Israel, it would have to put small children who have been separated from their parents, also kidnapped and raped, in cages, as if they were dogs." For Rodríguez, "The Dantesque images of small children locked in cages or of Jewish children handed over to the hands of Gazan children, who beat them with sticks, have no name or parallel, except in the Taliban world, which are the ideological cousins of Hamas." (47)

- It would be proportional to deliberately cause terror in children. "The face of horror and incomprehension of the Jewish child violently abused by Hamas children is unforgettable and unforgivable." Is it a proportional response from Israel to do the same in Gaza with its children? Unfortunately, Rodríguez continues. "The Arabs and the so-called Palestinians love death. A big difference between two towns that have grown together."

- If Israel has to respond proportionally to the massacre that Hamas has carried out among hundreds of young people, it would have to execute those who were celebrating a peace party in cold blood. Would a proportional response from Israel be to do the same with the youth of Gaza? ? The terrifying images of bodies riddled with bullets, kicked, stabbed and with shattered skulls are going around the world, but those blinded by anti-Jewish hatred will not see them and if they see them they will justify them. What would be Israel's proportional response to Hamas? Whatever it is, it will always be incomparable to the massacre that Hamas has wrought on Israeli society.

It seems that the so-called proportionality is only useful to the Palestinian terrorists who would benefit from a possible lower intensity of the Israeli attack.

The truth is that in the face of treachery, evil and sadism, it is difficult to ask victims to be careful not to affect the perpetrators too much.

In reality, the concept of proportionality is something absolutely different from what most people believe or understand.

Proportionality is the equation of the importance of the objective versus the cost of potential civilians who could be victims, that is, how significant the objective to be attacked is.(18)

Professor Ricardo Israel clearly explains in an article in INFOBAE "what he refers to is, nothing more and nothing less, that the level of force that must be used with respect to the level of resistance, that is, in no case is the army asked more powerful that does not use the means it has to win in the shortest possible time and taking care of the lives of its troops."(46)

And in practice, the Israeli army has confirmed that it is probably the most ethical in the world. As Professor Israel explains, "If it is about caring for lives, rather than preventing the use of the weapons that are available, the principle of proportionality refers to doing everything possible to warn civilians, with instructions to one's own soldiers to avoid harm to innocent non-combatants, warning them of what they intend to do. In that sense, "it is what is done when you notify of danger with leaflets that you are going to attack or bomb." There are not many armies in the world that warn their enemies where and when they are going to bomb, much less after having suffered the atrocities and barbarity that Hamas committed at the beginning of this Simchat Torah war.

· Of course Israel will not act with proportionality using human shields as Hamas does as described by the American Secretary of State, Anthony Blinken.

· "Hamas cynically and monstrously intentionally puts civilians in danger, hiding behind them, using them as human shields."(53)

· "Furthermore, Hamas's use of human shields, as well as any action aimed at preventing civilians from leaving danger areas, constitutes a blatant war crime. These types of practices clearly violate international law and humanitarian norms."

· So that there is no doubt. Ricardo Israel explains: "In any military action innocent people can suffer, but for that seeks the principle of proportionality is not "an eye for an eye", but rather, if there are consequences for civilians, these should not be the objective, but only "collateral damage", an expression that does not hide the suffering of innocents, but rather that this was not wanted or sought.

· "When analyzing possible collateral damage, it is essential to take into account the principle of proportionality. According to the laws of war, an attack can only be carried out if the anticipated collateral damage is proportional to the expected military advantage. In this context, the assessment of whether the neutralization of Hamas's military capabilities justifies the potential harm to civilians and civilian objects becomes crucial."

Pnina Sharvit in a document from the prestigious Spanish organization Acom states: "As for military attacks, international law establishes that it is permissible to direct attacks only against legitimate military objectives, such as Hamas bases, arsenals and training camps. On the other hand, "It is prohibited to directly attack civilians and civilian objects. A fundamental premise is the distinction between military and civilian targets, ensuring that only those sites that are clearly related to Hamas' military activities are attacked." And that is exactly what it does the army of the Jewish State.

· However, it is important to note that although there is no legal obligation to warn individuals before an attack, the laws of war establish an obligation to take practicable precautions to minimize harm to civilians. This implies that reasonable measures must be implemented to protect civilians to the extent possible. In this regard, Israel could give general warnings to civilians to leave areas where attacks are expected to take place.

· President Isaac Herzog specifies: "We have sent 6 million voice messages, 4 million text messages; "We have released more than 1.2 million pamphlets and made millions of calls before each bombing." (76)

· In relation to the situation in the Gaza Strip, it is necessary to clarify that it is not under Israeli occupation, since Israel completely withdrew from the region in 2005. However, Israel has the right, under international law, to impose a blockade on enemy territory, including a naval blockade.

In exceptional circumstances of severe humanitarian shortages, humanitarian aid agencies may request entry of aid and there would be valid reasons to consider this request.

It is clear then that Israel has acted in complete compliance with international norms and conventions that regulate war.

Chapter 22: Relatives of those kidnapped by the terrorist group Hamas Isis denounce the horrible situation they are experiencing

Background

It is difficult to believe but the war crimes of the Hamas-Isis terrorist group are so evident that in the past organizations and media that work on a clear, pristine and crystalline anti-Israeli agenda have been forced to denounce the horrible and appalling actions perpetrated in previous conflicts.

For example, the United Nations Human Rights Council (UNHCR) published a report in 2015 detailing violations of international humanitarian law and human rights by Hamas during the 2014 conflict in Gaza. The report mentions the indiscriminate and systematic use of rockets and mortars towards civilian areas in Israel by Hamas, endangering the lives of civilians. The use of civil infrastructure such as schools and hospitals for military purposes also stands out, constituting a breach of the neutrality and protection of these spaces.(78)

Even harder to believe

International Amnesty? An organization with a strong anti-Israeli agenda has documented the repression and human rights violations perpetrated by Hamas in Gaza.

Its reports have noted cases of extrajudicial executions and torture by Hamas against Palestinians accused of collaborating with Israel, as well as the violation of freedom of expression and association within territory controlled by the group.

And although it may seem incredible even to be absolutely hostile to the Jewish State, UNISPAL (United Nations Mission for the Middle East Peace Process) has carried out research on the impact of the conflict in Gaza and has documented cases of civilian casualties caused by the strategy of rocket launches and attacks launched by Hamas with indiscriminate targets towards populated areas of Israel, endangering the lives of Palestinian and Israeli civilians.

What is even more unusual is that even organizations funded solely to denounce Israel have been forced to denounce Hamas-Isis terrorism. Reports from the Independent International Fact-Finding Board (TIPH), which is an international organization established to monitor the situation in Hebron, has identified cases in which Hamas has harassed and harassed Palestinians who collaborate with or oppose Israeli organizations and authorities in their policies in Gaza.

Israel is such a liberal and open democracy that it allows NGOs openly hostile to the Jewish State to operate in Israel without restrictions.

These organizations such as "B'Tselem" and "Breaking the Silence" have documented testimonies and cases of abuses committed by Hamas in Gaza, including arbitrary arrests, summary executions and restrictions on freedom of expression and association.

The most important thing has been the leaked internal documents of the Hamas-Isis terrorist group.

In 2011, internal Hamas documents were leaked that showed corruption, abuses of power and human rights violations within the group.

These internal documents provided information on Hamas's internal practices and policies, including the repression of dissent and the violence carried out against its opponents.

Also important, have been reports from markedly and ostensibly anti-Israeli media outlets such as Al-Jazeera and Al-Araby Al-Jadeed, having reported and documented testimonies of Palestinians who have been victims of human rights violations by Hamas-Isis. These reports provide additional perspective and broaden the landscape of voices critical of Hamas' actions.

It is important to highlight that these sources and testimonies coming from what we could call the least hostile in the Jewish state provide a broader and more balanced vision of the situation in Gaza, and demonstrate the existence of criticism and concerns even within the population regarding the actions of Hamas. However, it is essential to recognize that there are also those in Gaza who support Hamas and support its terrorist actions against Israel, which emphasizes the complexity of the situation in the region.

These antecedents have served as a basis for the families of the more than 240 kidnapped people to denounce in courts and international organizations the barbarity they are suffering.(77)(78)

They have also gone to the governments of different countries to request help to bring back home the babies, boys and girls, men and women and older adults kidnapped by these monsters who have unfortunately shown that Never Again no longer exists, graphically. They have taught us that evil and sadism have no limits and that we must face reality, to survive as a Jewish State capable of protecting its citizens, we must put an end to this poisonous scourge, which is ultimately what the terror of Hamas-Isis represents. the paroxysm of evil. (79)(80)

Chapter 23: The Jewish people and Israel are resilient, they rise again despite horror and deep sorrow, AM ISRAEL JAI (The Jewish people live)

The history full of hardships, expulsions, murders, torture, crusades, inquisitions and a great Holocaust have not prevented the Jewish people from giving the world a better life, with a contribution in science, technology, medicine, philosophy, In art and in almost all disciplines, many Jews have stood out, obtaining - here if the concept fits - a disproportionate number of Nobel Prizes. Israel has granted society technological advances that allow us to simplify our existence and improve our comfort.

The blow of this brutal aggression has been difficult to assimilate, the wave of anti-Semitism has increased significantly, but Israel has proven to be able to overcome it, it did so in the pogroms before the creation of the state, it did so in the war of independence in which it almost 10 percent of Jews fell fighting, they did so in the '56 war and had the courage to attack assertively in the 1967 war.

In the 1973 Yom Kippur War, Israel lost more than 3,000 soldiers and the state was in danger of disappearing, recovering from the attacks on the Galilee that led to the Lebanon Wars.

Israel recovered from the massacres and kidnappings, from Munich, from Entebbe, from the expulsions of the Jews from Iraq and Yemen, from Syria and Lebanon, just as Israel was able to receive millions of Russian Jews and also the Jews of Ethiopia . The Jewish people have always recovered and Israel has always done so too.

It will be difficult to overcome this trauma just as it was the Yom Kippur War, but without a doubt the solidarity, the spirit and above all because there is no other alternative, to survive Israel must always win and it will do so.

AM ISRAEL (THE JEWISH PEOPLE VIVE).

C

Index

Bibliography

1   https://www.telemundo.com/noticias/noticias-telemundo/internacional/que-es-hezbollah-una-mirada-al-grupo-militante-respaldado-por-iran-que-rcna120452

2

Hezbollah. The party of God, its idiosyncrasies and its possible threat...https://ceeep.mil.pe/wp-content/uploads/2021/09/Hezbollah.-El-partido-de-Dios-su-idiosincrasia-y-su-posible-amenaza-global.pdf

3

What is Hezbollah and what is its military capacity? - SER chainhttps://cadenaser.com/nacional/2023/10/11/que-es-hizbula-y-cual-es-su-capacidad-militar-cadena-ser/?outputType=amp

4

Hezbollah - FDDhttps://www.fdd.org/issue/hezbollah/

5 https://www.idf.il/en/mini-sites/the-hamas-terrorist-organization/everything-you-need-to-know-about-hamas-underground-city[1]

6

When It Comes to Israel, Propaganda Trumps Facts
https://www.ynetespanol.com/global/opinion/article/byk1oakls

7

What is Hamas, the group that has ruled the Gaza Strip since 2007?
https://apnews.com/world-news/general-news-44c559f129fcf879727067e303940eehttps://www.infobae.com/america/opinion/2023/10/27/gaza-el-derecho-internacional-de-la-guerra-   and-proportionality/   avant-garde
testimony party

9

The harsh testimony of the survivors of the Supernova festivalhttps://www.lavanguardia.com/internacional/20231010/9289459/duro-testimonio-supervivientes-festival-supernova-vinieron-masacrarnos.amp.html

10

Direct witnesses to the Hamas massacre at a rave party in Israelhttps://www.eldebate.com/internacional/20231010/testigos-directos-fiesta-rave-masacro-hamas-xxxxx_145481_amp.html

11

Carles Villalonga La
Vanguardhttps://www.lavanguardia.com/autores/carles-villalonga.html

12

---

1.   https://www.idf.il/en/mini-sites/the-hamas-terrorist-organization/everything-you-need-to-know-about-hamas-underground-city-of-terror/

https://www.reuters.com/world/middle-east/german-israeli-woman-snatched-by-hamas-music-festival-is-dead-israel-says-2023-10-30/alertmundisl2rrss

Communication and Man
https://www.comunicacionyhombre.com > ...PDF

Terrorist propaganda and the media
13
https://www.youtube.com/watch?v=exBDBgMFn0k
14
https://www.clarin.com/mundo/quemados-atados-alambre-semanas-ataque[2]
appearing-corpses-israel_0_I09LjiHXVp.html[3]
mas-terrorist-organization/everything_you_need-to-know-about-hamas-underground-city-of-terror/[4]

15
ANDThe Israeli army shows the press images recorded by the body cameras of Hamas militants during the October 7 attack - BBC News World[5]
https://www.bbc.com/mundo/articles/c3g32e2g1pqo

16   https://www.iri.edu.ar/publicaciones_iri/IRI%20COMPLETO%20-%20Publicaciones-V05/Publicaciones/cd%20V%20congreso/ponencias/0%20Baz%E1n_Implicancias%20Estrat%E9gico-militares.pdf

17
The testimony of an Israeli who cannot find her family - Onda Cero
https://amp.ondacero.es/programas/mas-de-uno/audios-podcast/entrevistas/testimonio-israeli-que-encuentra-familia-ultima-noticia-son-gritos-mis-sobrinas_202310116526541be0d762000124e854.html

18
https://www.vozdeamerica.com/a/israelies-victimas-de-hamas-recuerdan-el-horror-del-ataque/7306785.html

19
The vanguard ://www.itn.co.uk/news/families-horrified-barbarity-hamas[6]

2.   https://www.clarin.com/mundo/quemados-atados-alambre-semanas-ataque-hamas-siguen-apareciendo-cadaveres-israel_0_I09LjiHXVp.html

3.   https://www.clarin.com/mundo/quemados-atados-alambre-semanas-ataque-hamas-siguen-apareciendo-cadaveres-israel_0_I09LjiHXVp.html

4.   https://www.idf.il/en/mini-sites/the-hamas-terrorist-organization/everything-you-need-to-know-about-hamas-underground-city-of-terror/

5.   https://www.bbc.com/mundo/articles/c3g32e2g1pqo

20

https://es.ara.cat/internacional/oriente-proximo/supervivientes-masacre-hamas-no-muertos-desaparecidos-hay-pueblo_130_4827040.html

21

43 minutes of images recorded by terrorists and their victims exhibit...

https://www.infobae.com/america/2023/10/23/43-minutos-de-imagenes-grabadas-por-terroristas-y-por-sus-victimas-exhiben-en-tiempo-real-la-masacre-ejecutada-por-hamas/?outputType=amp-typehttps://www.infobae.com/america/mundo/2023/10/27/la-brutalidad-de-hamas-en-primera-persona-el-relato-de-dos-testigos-a-tres-semanas-del-ataque-terrorista/

22

https://www.libertaddigital.com/espana/politica/2023-10-18/belarra-se-niega-a-condenar-el-ataque-terrorista-de-hamas-contra-ninos-mujeres-o-ancianos-israelies-7060038/

23

IDF publishes audio of Hamas terrorist calling family to brag about killing Jews https://www.timesofisrael.com/idf-publishes-audio-of-hamas-terrorist-calling-family-to-brag-of-killing-jews/amp/

24

https://www.libertaddigital.com/internacional/oriente-medio/2014-07-17/siete-razones-por-las-que-israel-tiene-derecho-a-defenderse-de-hamas-1276524075/25

A live massacre: images and testimonies detail the massacre of ...

26

https://www.france24.com/es/medio-oriente/20231025-una-matanza-en-directo-im%C3%A1genes-y-testimonios-detallan-la-masacre-de-ham%C3%A1s-en-israel

27

https://www.infobae.com/politica/2023/10/10/la-izquierda-volvio-a-reivindicar-los-ataques-terroristas-de-hamas-en-israel-la-reaccion-de-javier-milei/

28

https://www.libertaddigital.com/internacional/oriente-medio/2014-07-17/siete-razones-por-las-que-israel-tiene-derecho-a-defenderse-de-hamas-127[7]

---

6.   http://www.itn.co.uk/news/families-horrified-barbarity-hamas

7.   https://www.libertaddigital.com/internacional/oriente-medio/2014-07-17/siete-razones-por-las-que-israel-tiene-derecho-a-defenderse-de-hamas-1276524075/

29

https://pcchile.cl/2023/10/08/por-una-palestina-en-paz-y—de la-ocupacion-israeli/[8]

30

https://x.com/senador quintana/status/1710797945912648174?s=20

31

A live massacre: images and testimonies detail the massacre of ...

Una matanza en directo: imágenes y testimonios detallan la masacre de Hamás en Israel - Alerta Perú[9]

32

STATEMENT: Rep. Ocasio-Cortez on Violence in Israel and Palestine http://ocasio-cortez.house.gov/media/press-releases/statement-rep-ocasio-cortez-violence-israel-and-palestine

33

https://www.barrons.com/articles/lider-izquierdista-en-francia-genera-polemica-por-su-posicion-sobre-el-ataque-de-hamas-a845ed27

34

Sánchez goes to the Egyptian summit but neither calls nor plans to visit Israel - ABChttps://www.abc.es/espana/sanchez-cumbre-egipto-llama-piensa-visitar-israel-20231021220333-nt_amp.html

35

https://chile.shafaqna.com/ES/AL/1044538

36

Lula urges end to 'insanity of war' as Latin Americans killed in Hamas attack

https://amp.theguardian.com/world/2023/oct/11/lula-brazil-israel-hamas-gaza

37

https://www.swissinfo.ch/spa/israel-palestina_el l%C3%ADder-laborista-brit%C3%A1nico-afronta-una-rebeli%C3%B3n-en-sus-filas-por-su-defensa-de-israel/48923820

38   https://www.barrons.com/articles/hamas-war-shows-us-what-american-universities-stand-for-d[10]https://chile.shafaqna.com/ES/AL/1044538

39

Israel accuses part of the Government of Spain of aligning itself with... - EL PAÍS

https://elpais.com/espana/2023-10-16/israel-condena-energicamente-las-declaraciones-de-algunos-ministros.html?outputType=amp

40

https://www.telemundo51.com/noticias/local/manifestacion-pro-palestina-tras-medidas-del-gobernador-de-florida/2480057[11]/

8.   https://pcchile.cl/2023/10/08/por-una-palestina-en-paz-y-libre-de-la-ocupacion-israeli/

9.   https://alerta.pe/2023/10/25/una-matanza-en-directo-imagenes-y-testimonios-detallan-la-masacre-de-hamas-en-israel/

10.   https://www.barrons.com/articles/hamas-war-shows-us-what-american-universities-stand-for-d6b17314

11.   https://www.telemundo51.com/noticias/local/manifestacion-pro-palestina-tras-medidas-del-gobernador-de-florida/2480057/

41

https://www.nytimes.com/2023/10/13/us/university-of-pennsylvania-israel-palestine.html

43 https://www.nytimes.com/2023/10/13/us/university-of-pennsylvania-israel-palestine.html

44

https://docs.house.gov/meetings/FA/FA06/20230622/116138/HHRG-118-FA06-Wstate-NeuerH-20230622.pdf

45

https://unwatch.org/2022-2023-unga-resolutions-on-israel-vs-rest-of-the-world/

46

24075/https://www.libertaddigital.com/internacional/oriente-medio/2014-07-17/siete-razones-por-las-que-israel-tiene-derecho-a-defenderse-de-hamas-1276524075/[12]

47

https://aurora-israel.co.il/cual-seria-la-respuesta-proporcional-de-israel-a-hamas/

48

http://167.71.158.29/comunitarias

---

12.   https://www.libertaddigital.com/internacional/oriente-medio/2014-07-17/siete-razones-por-las-que-israel-tiene-derecho-a-defenderse-de-hamas-1276524075/

49

Hamas War Shows Us What American Universities Stand For - Barrons[13]
https://www.barrons.com/articles/hamas-war-shows-us-what-american-universities-stand-for-d6b17314

50   https://elpais.com/internacional/2023-10-27/el-conflicto-entre-israel-y-hamas-atiza-la-crispacion-en-las-universidades-de-estados-unidos.html
https://www.vozdeamerica.com/a/israelies-victimas-de-hamas-recuerdan-el-horror-del-ataque/7306785.html

51
https://www.bbc.com/mundo/articles/c3g32e2g1pqon

52   https://www.eldebate.com/espana/20231019/eurodiputada-belga-silencia-miembro-izquierda-unida-declaraciones-contra-israel_147573.html

53
https://www.google.com/amp/s/www.mediaite.com/news/blinken-recalls-how-hamas-gunmen-brutally-tortured-and-murdered-a-family-of-four-in-israel-and-then-sat-down-and-had-a-meal/amp/

54
https://www.latercera.com/opinion/noticia/columna-de-gabriel-zaliasnik-traicion-progresista/L4EYPDKVT5DU5OOO7P5RTET3WQ/

13.   https://www.barrons.com/articles/hamas-war-shows-us-what-american-universities-stand-for-d6b17314

55

https://www.enlacejudio.com/2023/10/31/bolivia-rompe-relaciones-diplomaticas-con-israel/

56

Colombia has returned its ambassador from Israel. President Gustavo Petro: "If Israel does not stop the massacre of the Palestinian people, we cannot stay there" Source Kann

57

GOVERNMENT CALLS THE CHILEAN AMBASSADOR TO ISRAEL FOR CONSULTATION FOR ATTACKS ON CIVILIANS IN GAZA

Through his official account of Carvajal."

Source La Nación

58

https://cnnespanol.cnn.com/video/bebes-asesinados-hamas-israel-cuna-familias-victimas-conclusiones-tv/

59

https://unwatch.org/whats-wrong-unrwa-must-reformed/

60

https://www.ynetnews.com/magazine/article/bj11r51ymt?utm_source=https://www.ynetnews.com&utm_medium=social&utm_campaign=general_share

61

⚠ MUST SEE - MAPPING THE MASSACRES: A geovisualization depicting the atrocities perpetrated by Hamas on Israeli lands on October 7.

This interactive map serves https://unwatch.org/comite-de-la-onu-condena-8-veces-a-israel-y-0-al-resto-del-mundo/as a tool for reflection and education, promoting awareness of the seriousness of the horrors: *https://bit.ly/49kjtmQ*

62

https://unwatch.org/comite-de-la-onu-condena-8-veces-a-israel-y-0-al-resto-del-mundo/

63

https://www.google.com/amp/s/www.infobae.com/america/mundo/2023/10/24/el-estremecedor-audio-del-llamado-de-un-terrorista-de-hamas-desde-un-kibutz-papa-mate-a-diez-judios-con-mis-propias-manos/%3foutputType=amp-type[14]

64

https://tn.com.ar/internacional/2023/10/24/mate-a-10-con-mis-propias-manos-el-aterrador-relato-de-un-miliciano-de-hamas-sobre-el-ataque-a-israel/

65

https://www.emol.com/noticias/Internacional/2023/11/01/1111634/hamas-chile-colombia-bolivia.html

66

https://www.newsweek.com/antisemitism-bds-natan-sharansky-3d-test-1461305

67

https://www.jcpa.org/phas/phas-sharansky-f04.htm

---

14.   https://www.google.com/amp/s/www.infobae.com/america/mundo/2023/10/24/el-estremecedor-audio-del-llamado-de-un-terrorista-de-hamas-desde-un-kibutz-papa-mate-a-diez-judios-con-mis-propias-manos/%3FoutputType=amp-type

68
https://www.gov.il/en/departments/general/behind_the_mask
69
https://shalom.cl/gabriel-silber/

70
https://eldiariojudio.com/2018/05/08/abu-mazen-el-invitado-de-piedra/

71
https://www.infobae.com/america/mundo/2023/11/01/un-funcionario-de-hamas-reivindico-la-masacre-de-civiles-lo-haremos-una-y-otra-vez-hasta-que-israel-sea-aniquilada/
72
https://www.state.gov/biographies/deborah-lipstadt/

73
https://jewishjournal.com/culture/295959/bernard-henri-levy-on-anti-semitism-the-diaspora-and-the-miracle-that-is-israel/

74 https://www.radiojai.com/index.php/2023/11/02/159316/el-antisemitismo-vuelve-de-la-mano-del-progresismo-alejo-schapire/
75
https://a-com.es/la-guerra-contra-hamas-aspectos-juridicos-basicos/

76
https://www.radiojai.com/index.php/2023/11/03/159352/antony-blinken-israel-no-solo-tiene-el-derecho-tiene-la-obligacion-de-defenderse
77
https://www.lagaceta.com.ar/nota/1009263/mundo/israel-denuncia-crimenes-guerra-hamas.html
78
https://www.lavanguardia.com/nacional/20231026/9332207/familiares-israelies-secuestrados-hamas-reclaman-madrid-ayuda-liberacion-inmediata-agenciaslv20231026.html
79
https://elcomercio.pe/mundo/europa/guerra-israel-hamas-familias-israelies-presentan-denuncia-por-crimenes-contra-la-humanidad-ante-la-cpi-gaza-palestina-franja-de-gaza-benjamin-netanyahu-ultimas-noticia/
80
Relatives of victims at the hands of Hamas file a complaint with the ICC for "crimes against humanity"[15]

---

15.   https://www.europapress.es/internacional/noticia-familiares-victimas-manos-hamas-presentan-denuncia-tpi-crimenes-lesa-humanidad-20231103184115.html

Book Summary

Last Black Saturday seemed to be a normal Shabbat in Israel. Simchat Torah was also celebrated, a festival that remembers that the Jewish people and through them, all humanity, received the Torah and particularly the ten commandments, given to Moses on Sinai. Very early in the morning the most brutal storm of blood and hatred in the history of the Jewish State broke out. Indeed, very close to the place where many of us believe that Moses was given what would later be the basis of justice and coexistence for a good part of humanity, the worst nightmare of the State of Israel and the greatest massacre of the Jewish people began. The closing of Auschwitz and the defeat of Nazi barbarism.

What we experienced that black Saturday is a horrible misfortune executed with treachery and malice in order to generate the greatest damage and fraud possible. Murders, rapes, burning of babies, kidnappings of children and the elderly, shootings and torture, and the whole range that human evil could imagine.

This book explores the history of the Pogroms, examines the different actors, their history and their responsibility and provides an accurate vision of how the chain of terrorism generated, organized and financed by Iran is related to its proxies Hamas and Herzbolla. It also addresses Israel's legitimate right to defend itself and the hypocritical response to the tragedy of a good part of the left and progressivism. It points out the double standard, hypocrisy and total lack of consequence of a good part of Western leaders and a significant percentage of the media regarding the treatment of the LGBT agenda, gender equality and religious freedom in Islamic countries. It also describes the appalling double standard of the United Nations and points out some of its inexplicable and absurd decisions.

This book is an agile and accurate instrument that tries to help understand the inexplicable.

While the Israeli army's operation called "Iron Sword" continues in response to the cruel and horrific massacre perpetrated by the terrorist group Hamas-Isis, an event that forever changed the Jewish State, this book is published with the high probability that said massacre has forever changed the Middle East and, quite possibly, will have a significant impact on the history of humanity.

Daniel Alejandro Farcas Guendelman

Biographical sketches

Studies and work life

He completed his studies at the University of Chile from where he graduated as a public administrator and graduated in Political Science.

In 1992, he obtained the President of the Republic Scholarship to pursue postgraduate studies in Spain, where he specialized in Business Administration at the Institute for Executive Development in Madrid.

He then pursued a Ph.D. in Leadership in Higher Education at Capella University, United States[1][16]

---

16.   https://www.bcn.cl/historiapolitica/#cite_note-0

He has completed postgraduate degrees in finance and marketing in the Specialization Programs in Management and Collaboration between Public-Private Sectors at the Institute for Public-Private Partnership in Washington.

Between 2002 and 2010, he was vice president and prorector of the University of Arts, Sciences and Communication (Uniacc) and rector of the IACC Professional Institute.

In 2009, he presided over the Corporation of As a teacher, he was a professor of the Training Program for Public Officials and the "Total Quality" workshop, both taught at the Faculty of Administrative Sciences of the SEK International University. He has also been a professor at the Seminar on Design of Marketing Strategies in Public Services at the School of Administration and Government of the Institute of Political Science of the University of Chile.

Since his arrival in Israel in 2021, he has been an associate professor at Bar Ilan University.

Political and public career

During his university days he was the general secretary of the Student Federation of the University of Chile.

He actively participated in the foundation and registration of the Party for Democracy[17]

During the government of the president Eduardo Frei Ruiz-Tagle[18], was appointed director of the Division of Social Organizations (DOS), dependent on the General Secretariat of Government ministry.

Between 2000 and 2002, he held the position of national director of the National Training and Employment Service (SENCE), during the government of President Ricardo Lagos Escobar.

He was director of the Antofagasta Health Services Company (ESMA) and the Maule Health Services Company (MERVAL).

In 2005, he became general coordinator of the government program of Michelle Bachelet, presidential candidate for the Elections of that same year.

In August 2013, he won as a candidate for deputy for District No. 17 in the primary elections held by the Nueva Mayoria coalition.

He was also Vice President of the Jewish Community of Chile.

Legislature 2014-2018

Deputy of the Party for Democracy[19] for District No. 17, Metropolitan Region, period 2014-2018, succeeding Maria Antonieta Saa Diaz[20].

17. https://www.bcn.cl/historiapolitica/redirect?url=/wiki/Partido_Por_la_Democracia

18. https://www.bcn.cl/historiapolitica/redirect?url=/wiki/Eduardo_Frei_Ruiz-Tagle

19. https://www.bcn.cl/historiapolitica/redirect?url=/wiki/Partido_Por_la_Democracia

20. https://www.bcn.cl/historiapolitica/wiki/index.php?title=Mar%C3%ADa_Antonieta_Saa&action=edit&redlink=1

Milton Keynes UK
Ingram Content Group UK Ltd.
UKHW051043020124
435341UK00011B/172